ARRANGING
FOOD
BEAUTIFULLY

ARRANGING FOOD BEAUTIFULLY

Tray and Steam Table Art

Susan E. Mitchell, CFE

JOHN WILEY & SONS, INC.

New York Chichester Weinheim Brisbane Singapore Toronto

This publication is designed to provide accurate and authoritative information in regard to the subject matter covered. It is sold with the understanding that the publisher is not engaged in rendering professional services. If professional advice or other expert assistance is required, the services of a competent professional person should be sought

Library of Congress Cataloging-in-Publication Data:
Mitchell, Susan E.
    Arranging food beautifully : tray and steam table art / Susan E.
Mitchell.
        p.   cm.
    Includes index.
    ISBN 0-471-28301-0 (cloth : alk. paper)
    1. Table setting and decoration.   I. Title.
TX879.M57   1999
642′ .8—dc21   98-45725

Printed in the United States of America

10 9 8 7 6 5 4 3 2 1

To all the artistic souls—

freelance food stylists, culinary consultants, roving chefs, recipe developers, food writers, cooking instructors, media spokespersons, cookbook authors, home economists, nutritionists—

all trying to make a living in this wild and crazy food industry that we so passionately love.

CONTENTS

PREFACE

Beasts feed, man eats; only the person of aesthetics and intellect knows, how to dine with all his senses.

Throughout history, certain aesthetic principles have been the basis of architecture, music, painting, and photography. These principles also apply to culinary masterpieces. They include focal point, balance, highlight or contrasts in color, unity, asymmetry and symmetry, texture, and, perhaps, the element of whimsy or pleasant surprise.

For example, a centerpiece of food or flowers is usually the focal point of a buffet line or table. The diner's eye should move from this artistic display toward the corners of the table. Steam table hotel pans, especially, deserve artistry in presentation. Catch the diner's eye with a jaunty, standout garnish. These little touches make a big impression.

The ancient Romans recognized the connection between an attractively decorated table and appetite. The cuisines of Asia have for centuries attached immense importance to the visual appearance of dishes.

These days, it's still important to please the eyes before the stomach, whether by the arrangement of food itself or the addition of simple edible adornments. Presentation raises the level of dining to that of an epicurean encounter. Creative touches make an artistic statement throughout the presentation—from the menu board to the grand finale.

While artful presentation seems to come naturally to some chefs, food stylists specialize in this area and have a great sense of composition, propping, and embellishment. My colleague, chef Marilyn Nergord of Coeur d'Alene's Capers restaurant, asked me, "Can visual creativity really be taught?"

My book is the answer to Marilyn's question. It features instructions, charts, culinary concepts from every menu category, food formulas for every part of the day, and examples from the industry as well as 32 how-to illustrations and 32 color photographs.

Each chapter describes a segment of the industry and its particular challenges. Garnishing and arranging ideas are central to the material, as are tips for propping the surrounding areas with fabrics, food, flowers, and distinctive dishware. Culinary concepts from seventeen years of consulting in the food industry are offered as an idea base. Signature successful formulas are followed with standardized recipes approved by a taste panel.

This book is meant as a reference and resource for people developing food presentation skills. My hope is that caterers, cafeterias, deli departments, school foodservice, in-plant feeders, hospitals, resorts, inns, and the military will delight in these easy garnishes that take merely minutes and cost pennies.

Even when corporate headquarters standardize the look of each product that meets the public eye, your style of design, arrangement, and garnishing can develop into a personal statement of your food philosophy. Arranging foods with favorite props or utilizing mainstream foods in an unusual way gives a signature stamp to your presentations. Expressing a theme with authentic props reflects your perception of art, ethnic cuisines, and style.

The basic point, which was ingrained in my training at Le Cordon Bleu in 1973, is, "Keep it simple rather than over-handled and very busy."

ACKNOWLEDGMENTS

I appreciate the number of manufacturers and distributors of smallwares/props, equipment, and food products who graciously lent or donated their products for photography; I also thank the models and photographers themselves:

Heather Bowen for her advice and creative brainstorming on food art direction in her lovely garden in Portland, Oregon, and Charles Jarrell of the San Antonio Arts and Cultural Affairs, for his research on the Flemish painting of "The Happy Family"

Plate 1 Nick Pupo, owner of PuPo's Produce of Spokane, Washington

Plate 2 JB Prince, garde manger tools, Oxo food styling tools, Dr. Delwyn Dick for his dental tools

Plate 3, 8, and 24 Brett Harrison for the use of photographs from my first book *30 Minute Meals*

Plate 4 Irene Daanen of Daanen's Deli for her assistance in obtaining props, cold cuts, and prepping, and for her overall moral support, and for reading each and every chapter and its variation; Gary Mazzone of Del Fin for the best deli trays on the market

Plate 5 Randy and Paula Johnson, Rockford Bay, Road 15, for their beautiful garden and plants; Paragon Marble, Hayden Lake, Idaho, for the great marble slabs on which I make so many recipes and presentations

Plate 6 Freddie Meyer and Jane F. Christie for the Oriental food and beautiful antique props

Plate 7 David Leong, owner of Food Service Distributors, for the seafood and the complimentary andouille; Molly Jones for her great energy and assistance in preparing the salad samplers

Plate 9 Tom Boge of Hearthbread BakeHouse, for his delicious rustic breads and rolls—I turned them into bread pudding in Plate 10.

Plate 10 Pier 1 in Spokane, Washington, and Allen Mastros for the star props; Chef Bill Steele, Pastry and More, for the gorgeous cake and cannoli; Caroline Collard for her fun culinary assistance and for bringing in a team from the Gourmet Club of the 3 C's (Cancer, Community, and Charity); Beverly Tyson for all her help, support, and phone calls in rounding up the cooking troops to prepare so many of the dishes for these photographs

Plate 11 Geri Hyatt, owner of The Rockford Bay Resort & Marina, for the use of her restaurant and deck

Plate 12 Cherry Marketing Institute for both the frozen and dried cherries; Tom Schreiber of Schreiber Spices for the quality spice samples to make all of my recipes tasteful as well as visual (the crew and neighbors loved it all!); Litehouse dressings and sauces

Plate 13 Larry Baker, store director of Tidyman's Grocery in Post Falls, Idaho, for letting us set up the equipment for a "real-location" soup bar/deli; Tony Barbagallo, who saved me with the proper props of soup tureens; angled cassoulet dishes with beautiful tile templates from Bon Chef

Plate 14 Zoopa's, a past client who lent a great overview photo I never wanted to art direct, prop, style myself

Plate 15 the perfect salad crocks from Templin's Resort, Post Falls, Idaho; ladles from Litehouse; hotel pan from Capers; Rice Tec, Inc. of Alvin, Texas, for the Jasmati, Basmati, and Texmati brown rice (a mere 25 pounds each)

Plate 16 Dan Jones (aka "Cabin-Dan") for lending his square jaw and torso as a model and the rest of his heart and muscles in support of the flagging author of this project; Mr. and Mrs. Art Thomasetti of Pulgini Pasta products, Fort Lauderdale, Florida, for their stunning rainbow-colored pastas; Mike Schneider, owner of Spokane Restaurant Equipment, Inc., for the unique hotel chafing dishes and modular steam table

Plate 17 Bally's Las Vegas Chef Tod Clore, for the initial tour, beautiful brunch shot, and helpful answers to myriad questions and reality checks

Plate 18 Craig Estabrook, region manager for Land O'Lakes, for all the cheeses and sweet butter (a whole case!); Athens Foods for large and small filo cups

Plates 19 and 20 Dan Jones for the use of his Couer d'Alene Lake cabin for two shots; Angela Geddis, proprietor of the Hayden Hideaway for the use of her star, heart, and clover bread molds—and a cozy cottage to live in last winter at Hayden Hideaway when I began this book

Plate 21, 22, and 23 Sandy Turner and Vickie Morris for their shopping and cooking and all the beautiful produce from their gardens; Allen Mastros, mountain pilot extraordinaire for all his shopping, propping, cooking the latkes, washing of many dishes, moving props all over, and especially for his moral support and for the use of his plane for both recreation and the cover shot

Plate 25 Chef Jesse Yoshida for the wok demo

Plate 26 Tony Barbagallo, who saved me with the proper props of angled cassoulet dishes with beautiful tile templates from Bon Chef; Carol Dingwall for her fine food styling assistance on this and other shots

Plate 27 Chef Marilyn Nergord, Caper's Restaurant; Caroline Collard and Georgeann Folk for the seashells; Brent Russell, great gourmet guy and oenophile from across the bay, who made my healthy version of Coquilles St. Jacques

Plate 28 John Grieve of Costal Marketing Consultants for the Clear Springs Trout

Plate 29 John Delport of Brakebush Brothers, Inc. for the chicken

Plate 30 Don Idiorne, vice president of Idaho Potato Commission; Bill McKay for the Angus beef loin

Plate 31 Rice Tec, Inc. of Alvin, Texas, for the Jasmati, Basmati, and Texmati brown rice; Art Thomasetti of Pulgini Pasta products, Fort Lauderdale, Florida; Tidyman's Grocery, Post Falls, Idaho, for the produce

Plate 32 Joy Wallace Catering Productions, Inc. for the experience of working with her great staff on yachts, at villas, and out in the gala tents for various south Florida parties. Thanks for the grand finale photo, where I enjoyed the presentation, arrangements, propping, garnishing, and flavors as a guest of the Schieffelin & Somerset Company press extravaganza

Don Boston for all of his help and friendly support in the whole process of testing recipes and running the photography project

Thanks also go to all of the Rockford Bay "babes" that helped so much and in so many ways on this book:

Jim and Kaye Fry for the use of their beautiful new home and kitchen in Rockford Bay and for Kaye's kitchen and design assistance; Geri Hyatt's creative art direction; Paula Johnson's private collection of props, her garden, and self as a model and first-run editor; Gaye Shumaker's supportive and continued friendship and editorial feedback early on—and for our great talks on women in business and food philosophy; Andrea Johnson

for her insights and chats on the sunny dock of Rockford Bay; and Carol
Bacon just for being her effervescent, upbeat self.

I appreciate in their own ways, my photographers Robert Johnson, Deni
Linhart, and especially the talent and professionalism of David Burch. The artist
and illustrator, Linda Fabrizius, has been wonderfully supportive throughout this
process and I value her continued friendship.

I'd also really like to thank Joan Watsabaugh of Profile Books, and Janet and
Harry Noe of Culinary & Hospitality Industry Publications Services (C.H.I.P.S.) for
first encouraging me to follow through on this concept as a very needed book for
this niche of the industry; and Executive Chef Chet Teel of the Main Street
Station in Las Vegas for his assistance and answers to myriad challenges in running a hot food line, beautifully and creatively!

Thanks to my mom for all her support in my freelance adventures and travels;
to Julia Child for writing back to me in 1970 and suggesting I study at Le Cordon
Bleu in London; to my dad for teaching me a love of Nature and foraging, and,
finally and especially, to Graham R. Rutherford for his phone and e-mail support
through the last six months of this project.

I hope I remembered to thank each one of the people who have helped see
this project through and I wish to continue to send them healing, white-light
energy in the future.

ARRANGING BUFFETS

1

PLANNING, PRESENTATION, AND PROPPING

To create a beautiful and appetizing tray, table, or hot line, weave the elements of art into your theme, menu, and party planning. Presentation and propping of the *entire* party should combine continuity and contrasts of color, texture, and shape or form, aromas and flavors, as well as foods served at different temperatures. Each chapter covers the presentation, arrangement, propping, and garnish (PAPG) of every dish, tray, buffet, and hot line. This approach covers more than just garnishing; it includes the overall presentation, food arrangement, surrounding props, and final garnishments.

The venerable art of decorating and presenting foods need not intimidate. Many food professionals find adding the final touches for a dish, deli platter, or even an entire buffet fun and artistic, a fitting send-off. Walking the line for the quality control checks is important to do before the guests arrive. Take a big handful of spoons and taste each dish; reseason if necessary. Look at your display as a first-time customer would and be sure the elements of art have been woven throughout.

Think of the entire menu, the buffet tables as well as each dish, as a composition. Plan a rhythm to your buffet or steam table line as well as a pattern to your platter. The dining experience should flow smoothly from one course or bite to another—and, of course, from one flavor to another.

The entire party should be completely planned. Develop a working script and job descriptions with duties and timelines for setup, demos, and breakdown for each employee. Layout of tables and trays, timetables, and backup plans for worst-case scenarios are good to have in mind, if not on paper, for when weather, equipment, or cooking challenges arise. Obtain good contracts, par sheets, and job duties and timelines from cooking colleagues (see Table 1, a sample par and rotation schedule).

Table 1. A Sample Par and Rotation Schedule.

Bakery Prep

Forecast:

Item	Container	Prep Batches	Prep Containers	Actual	Waste	Transfer	On Hand

Signature
Blueberry

Rotation #1
Cornbread-Plain
Cornbread-Pepperjack
Cornbread-Cheddar
Cornbread-Green Chili

Rotation #2
Bran-Honey
Bran-Pineapple
Bran-Raspberry
Bran-Banana Nut

Rotation #3
Peach Poppyseed
Cherry Nut
Zucchini
Carrot Pineapple
Apple Walnut
Peanut Butter

Table 1. *(Continued)*

Bakery Prep

Forecast:

Item	Container	Prep Batches	Prep Containers	Actual	Waste	Transfer	On Hand
Dessert Rotation:							
Gingerbread							
Bread Pudding							
Apple Crisp							
Orange Spice Cake							
Chocolate Chip Squares							
Blond Brownies							
Sauce Prep:							
White Sauce							
Honey Whip							
Herb Whip							
Red Sauce							
Pepperjack Cheese							
Red Onions							
White Onions							
Mushrooms							
Pudding Rotation:							
Tapioca							
Rice							
Jello							
Dressings:							
Ranch							
Creamy Herb Light							
Orange Cream							
Caesar							
Cleaning Schedule:							
Monday							
Tuesday							
Wednesday							
Thursday							
Friday							
Saturday							
Sunday							

Source: Zoopa's

Participatory and dynamic art or theater is enhanced by theme music, exhibition kitchens, costumes of servers and chefs, props, visual cues, and precise timing. Mixing the étouffée or jambalaya for Fat Tuesday from mise-en-place ingredients, flambéeing crepes, tossing a true Caesar salad, or whipping out omelets per guests' request shows culinary prowess and a sense of service and personal care.

The Multnomah Athletic Club was the source of a terrific planning template. This club is where chef Franz Popperl creates extraordinary menus and meals. I signed on for a short time and helped chef Popperl prepare dinner for Julia Child, Graham Kerr, and other luminaries during the last International Association of Culinary Professionals (IACP) Olympiad in Portland, Oregon. Here is their thorough form for completing catering, banquet, or party assignments; use it as an example.

—————— MULTNOMAH ATHLETIC CLUB ——————

Private Dining

Event Date: _____

Contact: _____   Event For: _____

Address: _____   Member: _____

Type of Function: _____   Address: _____

Room: _____

Phone/FAX: _____   Account #: _____

Arrival Time: 7:00 P.M. Departure Time: 12:00 A.M. Number of Guests: 85–100

Setup

Housekeeping and maintenance (show lists of items for each department)

Beverage and bar arrangements _____
    Charging method _____   Setup fee _____
    Number of stations: _____   bottles open _____   closed _____
    Cocktails, Glassware, Ice

Room Set/Special Requirements _____

Flowers _____

Menu*

5:00 P.M.: Band setup

7:00 P.M.: Reception
  Butler to serve house Chardonnay and have hosted bar open.
  22 dozen shrimp @ $28.00/dozen (16–20 shrimp per dozen)
  Pass shrimp w/tails and cocktail sauce on plate.

7:15 P.M.: Guest of honor to arrive.

8:00 P.M.: Food service for receptions
  Greek salad
  Fruit display
  Rice pilaf
  Whole green beans with garlic, onion, and tomato
  Baron of beef with potato rolls
  2 breasts of turkey with potato rolls
  Band to play soft music as guests arrive.

8:30 P.M.: Dancing
  Cake by MAC; cake to read: Greatest Lover, Husband and Father in the World

Other

Table

Votive candles

Mirrored tiles

Cloths (white)

Napkins (white)

Cutlery, Crockery

Calligraphy

Entertainment

7:00–11:00 P.M.: Windfall (setup 5:00 P.M.)

Flowers: by client

Cake: by MAC

Fees

Date booked _____

Confirmed by _____

Room charge _____

Equipment _____

Purchase order # _____

Notes

Client will deliver Lebanese items Saturday A.M. Signs will be placed on items noting what they are and waiver will be signed.

Servers to have hummus out as guests arrive.

50 percent deposit required 7 days prior to function.

Guaranteed number of guests must be confirmed 72 hours prior to event.

If cancellation occurs for any portion of this order within 5 business days prior to your event, you will be charged for the full amount.

All food and beverages subject to 17 percent service charge.

*Note to chef: As last year, client will bring in three Lebanese Dishes, (all delivered Saturday A.M.)—hummus with pita bread, kibbee (needs to be heated), meat in phyllo.

CLIPBOARD   CHEF   BANQUETS   CLIENT   BEVERAGE   BAR   STAFF   ACCOUNTING

Always be prepared for the unexpected. Many caterers check their lists thrice and bring backup equipment. Storms or winds may come up in the middle of your event. Chefs have cooked in snowstorms in hooded parkas and hung onto tents blowing in the wind. Yachting chefs have battened down the hatches and food in a gale storm on the sea and chefs on land have patched up wedding cakes smashed by reckless drivers rounding corners in a hurry. So, do bring in extra icing, flowers, pastry bags, and any other item needed to freshen and garnish each dish.

Add personal touches, photographs, garnishes, and gifts that will differentiate you from your competition. The visual aspects of food arrangement and garnishing are like sculpture and painting. A still life of cheeses and fruits on marble, for example, enhances the pleasure of dining well by pleasing the eye as well as the palate. Serving not just a half pan of rice pilaf but shaping it into a molded timbale or pyramid adds height and visual appeal.

Planning parties and menus, pairing ingredients, juggling flavors, and achiev-

I experienced one beautiful event—well, two, actually—with Joy Wallace Catering Productions of Miami. Schefflin and Associates, an advertising agency, puts on extravagant press trips all over the country to promote their clients' liquors and liqueurs. All the writers, at this festivity, were bused from the trendy Delano Hotel to the swamps to see an alligator wrestling show, then took airboats to a little island, where we saw a phenomenal swamp food presentation replete with whimsical thematic props and authentic dishes. The jaded writers shook their heads in disbelief at the huts full of delicious, colorful foods and costumed laughing servers—apparently in the middle of nowhere. Joy herself, a tall titian-haired bundle of energy, played her part with enthusiasm and received hearty accolades.

She outdid herself that very night at the Villa Vizcaya at a black-tie farewell dinner. Here, gondolas brought us all in to a Renaissance villa with enormous balconies, meandering paths, whispering waterfalls, and moonlit gardens. As on the swamp islands, there was no kitchen or refrigeration. I, of course, peeked behind the scenes to see how Joy orchestrated the event. Chefs and their assistants were barbecuing like mad and turning out tasty little crown racks of veal. I was so impressed I worked for Joy part time through the holiday season later that year and had great fun creating buffet tables of props, foods, and garnishes on the yachts she catered to.

Joy Wallace's food philosophy is to never compromise on standards of food quality. She would rather lose money than cut corners. The creativity of her team has its source in the four menu designers on staff and the three full-time chefs. If you're ever in Miami, try to go to one of her parties; give her a call at 305-252-0020.

---

ing resonance between ingredients and final adornments is vital. For presentation, potential focal points and props could include:

Distinctive baskets	Jagged marble slabs
Tiered stands	Terra-cotta vases
Figurines	Bric-a-brac
Lamps	Candles
Tapestries	Serapes and fabrics
Creative menu listings	Hanging mobiles
Flags and banners	Wine bottles and casks
Mirrored trays	Pedestals/risers of various heights
Flower bouquets	Ice, tallow, or salt dough carvings
Table underliners	Tablecloths, ruffles, and drapes

Thematic props may be obtained at garage sales, auctions, antique stores, kitchenware shops, department and import stores, catalogs, and estate and liquidation sales.

Broken pieces of marble add rustic texture and interest. Corian, however, is lighter and more manageable than marble. Go to marble, granite, hardware, or home stores for scraps, samples, or castaway tile or marble pieces for unique platter presentations.

If you have friends that love garage sales and antiquing, tell them that you're looking for props. Let them do the footwork, bring back the deals, and show you their prizes. Many towns have a collectibles club. Join or simply ask for information on where the good buys are. Members would love to go on a prop-shopping hunt for you. Simply explain the boundaries and the budget.

Customers can supply their own platters for more elegant food arrangements. If your trays are used, ask for a deposit. This assures the return of singular serving dishes you purchase from local and national vendors.

Informational props include clever menu copy, chalkboards, and little labels. Let the diners know if a dish is from a signature formula or personally developed recipe, heart healthy, vegetarian, or a reputed aphrodisiac. Staff members who can do calligraphy should be exploited. Supply cartoons; offer a free drink for the right answer to a "question of the day." Note a special affirmation of the day, season, or holiday, or raise a philosophical question.

Remember to have a focal point, whether a large spray of flowers on a table, a tray with one grand garnish, or a hot line hotel pan Southwest item scattered with minced colorful bell peppers. See Chapter 2 for many more garnishes to feature on trays and steam table lines. Whatever the dish, make sure the items are matched and arranged, as well as garnished, in compatible colors and flavors. Individual flavors should shine on their own and not mask one another or fight for attention.

(This is also true for texture in an accompaniment dish. Balance soft foods with crunchy foods and vary their form and shapes. This is easily done by turning a vegetable or molding a salad or rice dish into a variety of forms. Balancing textures, colors, forms, and flavors is essential to good menu and party planning and presentation. You are developing an artistic culinary masterpiece that addresses all of the senses—not just vision.)

Base focal points on the theme or style of the party, menu, or dish. Props should enhance the food rather than overwhelm it. You can simply arrange a few ingredients, as an adornment atop the tray or steam table pan.

The food, not the platter it's on, should be the visual draw. Of course, the tray or steam table pan can add interest without distracting from the natural beauty of the food; unusual pans, like oval chafing dishes with copper handles, are attractive in this way. All of the props—music and costumes included—should add to the pleasure of the foods without overwhelming or detracting from them.

Finally, the most beautiful buffet line will deteriorate if the foods are not kept properly hot or cold. Nestle's corporate chef Jim Harvey advises, "Synergy is very important in buffets, between the equipment design, layout, food presentation and arrangements." For more information on equipment and chafers, see Chapter 6.

MISE EN PLACE AND ORGANIZATION

Organization is key to good cooking and presentation. The kitchen itself must be designed to facilitate the menu and work flow. When a kitchen designer/chef works with the architect on kitchen plans from the outset, a well-equipped and arranged kitchen is a likely outcome. Kitchen planning is too often an after-thought in our industry and chefs must work within the confines of architectural ignorance. Space- and time-saving devices that help order storage and work flow are, however, becoming more available.

Organize your prop closet by theme or holiday event. Large clear plastic bins may be a storage help. Arrange linens, fabrics, and table skirts by color. Just a few colors of tablecloths are needed for holiday theme parties. Have dedicated shelving for special glassware, vases, and silk flowers.

Look for plastic bins that fit well on top of each other. Install foot pedals that open reach-ins when your arms are full, faucet pedals, minimal-space storage containers, hanging racks, and handy shelves. Work with your suppliers to identify space-saving equipment and—why not?—planet-friendly kitchen products.

Hunting for mislaid utensils and ingredients is not only time-consuming but frustrating, so give time and attention to mise en place—the putting in place—before proceeding with recipes and presentations. This encourages a smooth cooking rhythm instead of an irritating scramble. When cooks work together in a well-ordered kitchen, their activity becomes almost a dance.

Professional cooks and chefs work efficiently because they understand and follow principles of organized cooking. Every needed ingredient, garnish, and utensil is conveniently placed so that the work will flow smoothly.

Read recipes thoroughly. Check that all ingredients have been delivered and are in good condition.

At home, simply play with your food; experiment with new cuts and shapes. Many vegetables and fruits look great when cut in half to show the patterns of the interior.

Practice new techniques in advance. Measure ingredients and lay them out in order of use. You can make good use of this strategy during off-peak hours by slicing, chopping, and otherwise preparing weighed and portioned ingredients. Use zip-closing plastic bags for prepared and measured ingredients. Tray it all on covered sheet pans and slide into the reach-in until it's time to arrange and garnish the food, be it platter or heated steam table items.

An excellent summary of work flow principles is the classic "Kitchen User's Guide" from David Larousse's book, *The Professional Garde Manger:**

- If you open it, close it.
- If you get it out, put it away.
- If you turn it on, turn if off.
- If you move it, put it back.
- If you spill it, wipe it up.
- If you get it dirty, clean it up.
- If you unlock it, lock it up.
- If you break it, get it fixed.
- If you care about it, treat it as your own.

EDIBLE DECORATIONS

These easily accessed lists present colorful garnishes that can quickly decorate foods, trays, and buffet tables. See Color Plate 1 for a large group of fruits and vegetables organized by color.

Always keep an eye out for baby greens and esoteric greens—fiddlehead ferns, flowering herbs, foraged edible plants. Remember that roots and tubers hold up best on steam tables and platters. Acorn squash and deep-fried potato roses hold up particularly well. The inside leaves of stalks and lettuces make fine edible vessels. Many of these fruits and vegetables may be readily and smoothly sliced, diced, julienned, or shredded. Alternatively, they may be cut into stars, hearts, or flowers to cascade down the surface of the dish. Remember white space can be an element of contrast, too, with the plate, tray, or "prop" showing through. Let the intrinsic beauty of the dish itself create negative space for the food ingredients.

Lists of All Produce by Color

Greens

Vegetables

Asparagus   Broccoli

Blue Lake green beans   Brussels sprouts

*Published by John Wiley & Sons, Inc., © 1996.

Cabbage, regular, napa, and savoy

Cactus leaves; tomatillos

Cardoons; artichokes

Celery and celery hearts

Cucumbers

Fennel; sorrel; watercress

Greens, a copious assortment

Green acorn squash; chayote

Green chiles; green bell peppers

Green onions; leeks

Herbs

Kale

Kohlrabi

Lettuces, various types

Lima beans

Long beans

Okra

Snow pea pods; sugar snaps

Sprouts of all types

Zucchini; patty pan squash

Fruits

Apples

Asian pear

Avocados, Hass and Florida

Cherimoyas

Fresh Calimyrna figs

Granny Smith, Pippin apples

Green prickly pears

Gooseberries

Guavas; feijoas

Honeydew melon (inside slices)

Kiwi; kiwano/horned melon

Limes; limequats

Pears, Anjou and Bartlett

Plantains (with peel)

Thompson/Perlette Grapes

Purples

Vegetables

Beets

Eggplant

Purple bell peppers

Purple kohlrabi

Purple pearl onions

Purple potatoes

Purple (red) cabbage

Purple sage

Purple salad savoy

Red onions

Royal Opal basil

Turnips

Fruits

Black Mission figs

Blueberries

Boysenberries

Grapes, Concord, Red, and
    Champagne (tiny)

Plums; passion fruit

Oranges and Yellows

  Vegetables

Banana and other yellow chiles

Butter beans

Carrots, baby carrots

Cherry, pear yellow tomatoes

Corn, baby corn

Orange jalapeños

Orange and yellow bell peppers

Rutabagas

Squash, banana, butternut, crookneck, golden acorn, golden
nugget, spaghetti, and sunburst

Sweet potatoes

Yellow cucumber

Yellow Finn potatoes

Yellow wax beans

Yukon Gold potatoes

  Fruits

Apples

Apricots

Asian pears

Bananas (skin on)

Babaco; tangerines

Cantaloupe; Crenshaw melon

Carambola or starfruit

Golden Delicious apples

Grapefruit

Kadota figs

Kiwano/horned melon

Lady apples

Oranges, lemons, kumquats

Papayas; mangoes

Peaches; nectarines

Persian melons

Persimmons

Pineapples, interior

Pumpkins

Quince

Yellow cherries

Yellow raspberries

Yellow tamarillos

Yellow watermelon

Reds

  Vegetables

Beets

Cranberry beans

Pimiento

Red bell peppers

Red chiles

Radicchio

Radishes

Red-leaf lettuce

Red potatoes (skin on)

Red Swiss chard

Rutabagas

Tomatoes, cherry, roma, beefsteak

Fruits

Blood oranges	Red apple varieties; crab apples
Cherries	Red bananas (skin on)
Cranberries	Red Bartlett, Stark Crimson pears
Currants	Red prickly pears
Grapefruit	Red tamarillos
Grapes	Rhubarb
Loganberries; thimbleberries	Spiced apples
Plums	Spiced pears
Pomegranates (whole and seeds)	Strawberries
Raspberries	Watermelon

Whites

These hues contrast with both colorful and dark-hued products.

Bean sprouts	Jicama
Button squash	Leeks (white part only)
Cauliflower	Mushrooms
Celery root	Onions (white)
Chinese cabbage	Parsnips
Daikon	Potatoes, interior
Garlic	Turnips
Ghost pumpkins	Water chestnuts
Horseradish, interior	White cabbage; radishes

Blacks and Browns

Vegetables

Eggplant	Potatoes

Fruits

Blackberries	Figs, cut into tulips or sliced in half
Cherries	Ginger, julienned and deep fried
Coconut, exterior	Grapes
Dates	Kiwi and pineapples, exterior

Dried and Preserved Fruits and Vegetables

Dates

Dried cranberries, blueberries,
    cherries, and tomatoes

Hot chiles

Mild chiles

Olives, ripe, green, stuffed,
    imported

Pickles

Raisins, sultanas

Edible Flowers

Keep all flowers dry; do not rinse them. Most of the fragile flowers are best used as a confetti cut-up, to scatter over arrangements and food presentations. The most flavorful of flowers are usually the most fragile.

Store all flowers at 34°–38°F. Most keep 3–7 days. Check boxes of flowers as they come in and wipe out any condensation. Keep flowers in box with lightly damp paper towel. Wipe out extra moisture from time to time.

These flowers, whole or chopped, provide brilliant color to food arrangements served at any time of day. *Make sure all flowers are unsprayed!*

More Ideas for Special Effects

Float edible flowers in vinegar creations for extra color.

Add minced nasturtium petals and leaves to omelets, tuna fish, or deviled-egg mixtures for a bright yellow hue and peppery flavor.

Dip squash or pumpkin blossoms in cornmeal or beer/flour batter or stuff with cheese and lightly fry.

Mince any combination of edible flowers and add to cheese spreads, herb butters, and batters for waffles, pancakes, and crepes.

Float borage sprigs, which taste like cucumber, in cool summer drinks and toss in salads.

Sprinkle chive blossoms on salads, vegetables, and other egg dishes for subtle onion flavor. Bachelor buttons give the same visual effect without the onion flavor.

Calendula petals imbue sauces with a beautiful yellow-orange hue.

Flowers from any herb plant taste just like the herb itself.

Marigolds and snapdragons stand up well to heat and don't wilt so easily, which make them great for steam tables and hot trays.

For desserts, crystallize pansies, angelica, Johnny-jump-ups, and roses in sugar and use to garnish cakes or pastries.

Edible and Decorative Flowers and Foliage

Flowers	Season	Life Span
Common	year round	7–10 days
Carnation		
Mini-carnation		
Fillers		4–7 days
Artichoke		
Ornamental kale		
Zucchini flowers		
Greens	year round	7–10 days
Chives		
Dandelion		
Dill		
Rosemary		
Holland	spring and fall	4–6 days
Tulips		
Gerbera daisy		
Lilies		4–6 days
Day lily		
Oriental tiger lilies		
Roses	year round	4–6 days
Madame Delbard		
Assorted colors		
Tropical	year round	7 days
Gardenia		
Ginger		
Hibiscus		
Orchid		
Passion flower		
Wild	summer	4–6 days
Daisy		
Sunflower		

More Flowers and Foliage to Choose From

Acacia flowers—golden yellow

Angelica—herb of the parsley family, imparts green color and flavor to confections/liqueurs

Anise—feathery bright green leaves

Apple buds—white delicate flower from the apple tree

Arugula—dark green leaves with tiny spikes of white edible flowers

Bananas—blossoms and leaves

Bay leaves—from the evergreen tree

Bee balm/bergamot—flowers of pink, magenta, purple, white, and scarlet

Begonia—from your window sill

Blue and pineapple sage—sweet, flavorful, and beautiful

Borage—distinct cucumber flavor, star-shaped sky-blue flowers

Broom and Scotch broom—in gold

Burnet—delicate green leaves and pink flowers

Calendula—cut up petals and scatter for best effect

Carnations—readily available in a rainbow of colors

Chamomile—small plant with daisylike flowers

Capers—pickled flower buds of the caper plant

Chervil—fernlike leaves and clusters of tiny white flowers

Chile pepper plants—all colors, very sturdy

Chives and blossoms—mauve-colored edible flowers

Citrus flowers—from lemon, orange, or lime trees

Clary sage—herb of the mint family

Clovers—assorted sizes and colors

Costmary—herb with a minty taste, but bitter overtones; use sparingly

Cowslips—also known as primroses

Daisy—no real flavor but sturdy for garnishing

Dandelions—flowers, leaves, and roots

Daylilies, including tiger lilies—shades of yellow, apricot, and burgundy

Dianthus—pinks—bright pink flower

Dill—fine-textured foliage with delicate yellow edible flowers

Elderflowers—symbolize beauty

Elderberries—blackish-purple berries used for soups, jellies, and wine

Fennel—green or bronze foliage with flat-topped clusters of yellow flowers

Fuchsia—not usually available at retail; easy to grow your own

Geranium—colorful confetti petals; leaves have scents of mint, rose, and fruit

Globe amaranth—retains color when dried

Hawthorne—blossoms and berries

Hollyhocks—to stuff

Honeysuckle—a symbol of fraternal love

Hyssop—6-inch spikes of tiny white, blue, or pink edible flowers

Jasmine—aromatherapeutic

Iceland poppy—petals and seeds

Lavender—spikes of tiny pink, white, purple, and lavender flowers

Lemon balm—scalloped leaves and small white edible flowers

Lemon verbena—diminutive heliotrope-scented flowers

Lilac—in a rainbow of colors

Lovage—hollow stems with celerylike leaves and flat tiny yellow flowers

Marjoram—rounded clusters of pink and mauve flowers in late summer

Marigolds (Mexican)—1-inch clusters of golden flowers

Mints—many kinds; purple, pink, and white flowers in midsummer

Nasturtiums—2-inch red, yellow, mahogany, orange, or cream flowers

Orchids—great on foods as well as in drinks

Oregano—minuscule white edible flowers in late summer

Pansies—subtle, but every color has a different flavor

Passion flowers—last but a day; use the fruit!

Peonies—petals or the whole voluptuous bloom

Rosemary—especially the flowers

Safflower—crocus with orange-red stigmata

Sage—variegated greens and purple leaves, tiny lavender flowers

Savory—summer, pinkish-white flowers; winter, dark, glossy leaves

Snapdragons—colorful little blooms that hold up well

Sorrel—garden, English, broadleaf

Squash blossoms—all varieties

Sunflowers—another daisy

Sweet cicely—fernlike leaves and 2-inch clusters of little white flowers

Sweet woodruff—great for garlands

Tansy—rather strong-smelling leaves and bright yellow flowers

Thistles—handle carefully

Thyme—attractive white, purple, and pink flowers in midsummer

Tulips—colorful edible containers as well as versatile garnishes

Violas and violets—frost or candy the colorful flowers for longer shelflife

Yucca—plant and blossoms

TECHNIQUES FOR DECORATION

Garnishing food can indeed be easy and fun. Color, shape, form, and texture are as important in food presentation as in any artwork. Aroma and flavor are a bonus. Put simply, garnishing is the use of the color, shape, and texture of simple foods to enhance the appearance of a dish. Finishing touches can raise an otherwise ordinary dish to the level of edible art.

For example, you can emphasize color by placing an intensely green herb sprig on a pale, spring-green, creamy soup. Place the sprig of oregano or watercress at a jaunty angle or perhaps on a thin slice of lime, and add a contrasting dollop of sour cream. Enhance a baked noodle casserole by topping it with slices of the prevailing cheese cut in hearts, spades, or triangles; scatter cubes of contrasting cheeses as well. Carrot and parsnip curls or shreds hold up in heat; toss them over stews containing these sturdy ingredients. Give scrambled eggs an intriguing look with a fresh melange of minced fresh herbs and edible flowers folded in before service. For a little herbal aromatherapy, tuck a clump of whole fresh or dried herbs in the back corner of the chafing dish.

In choosing the garnishes, think of the final plate presentation as an artistic composition. You may wish to create a diagram or quick sketch of the placement, size, and shape of foods. Practice on a platter first, so the final moments before service or send-out go smoothly. Make one plate exactly how you want it for others to copy. This is the prototype or "hero" for chef underlings to follow.

Use one unusual element to catch the eye—a bright color, a surprising shape, an esoteric food. Contrast colors and juxtapose textures. If you are garnishing a dish with a sauce, use in the sauce or atop the finished dish raw vegetables, fruits, herbs, or flowers—or an item that is called for in the recipe, but cut it into an interesting shape.

Experiment with the new, brilliantly hued vegetable powders, such as beet, spinach, and rich, dark-brown mushroom. Use them either as powders or liquefied for sauce art. Search for sources of suppliers for the fruit powders as well, including raspberry; these make beautiful rainbow food garnishes.

The powders can be dusted inside an etched leaf or teardrop of chocolate on a dessert plate. Executive chef Franz Popperl, CEC, CCE, now at the Multnomah Athletic Club, and his pastry chef, Christopher Harris, shared a number of dessert ideas that use berry powders and chocolate dessert powders. And best of all, the desserts plate easily. For these and other culinary concepts of this genre, read the dessert section of Chapter 3.

For savory embellishments, simply wash and process or mince parsley for a quick and easy universal garnish to have on hand. Wring parsley in cheesecloth or a dishtowel. (Prepare plenty, as it refrigerates and freezes well.) Sprinkle this bright green finish down the center or diagonally across a savory entrée dish or hotel pan.

Another simple but colorful garnishing idea is to sprinkle a diagonal coating of walnuts, toasted coconut, golden raisins or currants, and brown sugar over a half or full hotel pan of oatmeal. This contrast of textures enlivens a notoriously dull-looking breakfast food.

Casseroles may benefit from the same approach—use sieved egg yolk, chopped egg white, and minced parsley—for the same reason. Watercress in two small bunches to the sides of the food is more interesting than the traditional small bunch of whole parsley.

Use the corners of the serving pan or chafing dish for scoops of hummus with a cluster of Italian parsley centered with marigolds, nasturtiums, or a sprig of var-

---

An example of contrasting colors and textures is seen at the Treasure Island Hotel in Las Vegas, headed by chef Kenneth Weiker, who has a whole wall of garnishes in hotel pan displays for easy reference. Weiker trains his staff to scatter scallion fans and pineapple chunks over sautéed pork in sweet-and-sour sauce, for a contrasting finish. In the back of the hotel pan is a fresh pineapple garnish, including the bright green top and large wheels of sunny sliced fruit with its rough-textured peel.

At the feasts that I attended in Tblisi in the Republic of Georgia with the San Diego chapter of the American Culinary Federation (ACF), cilantro plants were part of an edible centerpiece, along with black opal basil for guests to pluck at will and add to their plates as a garnish. The tables were long and narrow, groaning with an abundance of appetizers, "small plates," and condiments. What with stand-up toasts, drinking out of a horn, and much ribaldry, the meals served up great food and energy reminiscent of the food orgies of days gone by.

iegated kale. Alternatively, decorate corners with chrysanthemums of red onion for heartier entrées, chili pepper flowers for Mexican dishes, and citrus flowers for seafood entrées.

A speedy and attractive way to garnish sweet potatoes is to cover the pan completely with toasted coconut. A military culinary colleague avoids garnishing the food altogether and bravely sprinkles colorfully dyed raw rice on the runners between the inserts of hotel pans instead. Par-cooked rice is even better, so there is no danger of guests cracking their teeth on it. It could easily and inadvertently get from the runner into the food.

If you have a little more time, garnish with julienned or diced bell pepper of every color, chopped flowering herbs, or minced purple and white kale. This approach charms through its air of disheveled nonchalance.

Elements of the dish presented in different or larger forms also make for an aesthetic finish. If roasted corn is a prominent ingredient in a recipe, for example, place a spray of baby corn in the corner or maybe the center of the hotel pan or chafing dish in which the food is served. A flower of red or green bell pepper in a corner of the pan is the classic garnish for dishes containing peppers.

Traditional garde-manger work and vegetable sculpting involves tedious and time-consuming handiwork. Much of the time dishes treated this way look as if the cook has overhandled them. Some chefs decry the passé use of inedible tomato roses while other chefs don't think anything is edible or stylish about a turnip or raw rutabaga rose, especially when it's dyed a bright neon color.

Remember this simple rule: The garnish should be edible and complement the flavors of the dish. It should not exist for its beauty alone.

Garnishes should hardly ever be stuck in the middle of food but rather to the side. Further, the Zen concept of white space leads to minimalist, clean-looking, uncluttered garnishes. Often, colorful components of a dish stand on their own without need for embellishment. Consider negative space for the most pristine arrangement or look of all; many times the platter or tray itself makes a beautiful frame around the food.

Many simple garnishes are used creatively in other countries. Cilantro, or Chinese coriander, is used in many cultures and cuisines to enhance a dish. This humble herb can act as ingredient, presentation, or striking garnish. The cuisines of Mexico, China, and the Republic of Georgia utilize this versatile herb in myriad ways.

These days, edible art lends aesthetic appeal to everything from deli trays to hot lines. Your guests will enjoy walking the line or buffet just to appreciate your attention to detail and decoration.

FRUIT AND VEGETABLE GARNISHES BY CATEGORY

Many garnishes require a soak in ice water for freshening; this also preserves the garnish for a day or two. For longer storage, submerge garnishes in iced water and freeze for as long as ten months. Have a garde-manger day and make heaps of garnishes to draw from deep-freeze storage when needed.

Go gently, calmly, and carefully as you begin to learn. With practice, your skill will increase rapidly, along with your culinary prowess. This approach to cooking is not only fun and satisfying but also your guests and food friends will be impressed and your new expertise may command a higher salary.

Citrus Fruits

Carving Tools (see Color Plate 2)

Small paring knife for lemons and limes

Medium to large kitchen knife for oranges and grapefruits

Grooving and grapefruit knives, striper, and zester for star patterns

Plain or grooved cutters to remove flesh from skin

Cartwheels, Twists, Fans, and Scalloped Edges for Platters

Peel a lime, lemon, orange, and grapefruit in alternate strips with a stripper or small peeler (see Figure 1). Slice the fruit thin and cut each slice halfway from on edge to the center. Turn in opposite directions for a pinwheel effect, as shown in Figure 2.

Add a sprig of watercress on either side of citrus slices for a final, colorful artistic touch. Alternatively, place a spray of sprouts behind wheels to symbolize the rays of the sun.

FIGURE 1. **Vertical stripper peeling citrus fruit (Some tools have stripper and zester on one unit.)**

For fans, overlap three to five half slices in the form of a fan. Garnish the juncture of the fan with angelica, candied violet, truffle slices, a pepper star or diamond, or contrasting melon ball (see Figure 3).

To scallop the edge of a dish, place citrus halves in a long line with the cut halves facing each other, but not dead on. The asymmetry adds interest. Figure 4 illustrates this effect clearly.

Coronets, Chrysanthemum Flowers, Baskets

For a citrus crown or coronet, mark the center of the fruit so that it may be cut evenly. Using a pointed knife, make zigzag cuts right through the middle. (Use a very sharp fluter for softer fruits and vegetables.) Then simply stab the fruit to the center. Carefully separate the two halves (see Figure 5). Cut a thin slice of the base so each coronet is stable. Remove the pulp, if desired, with a grapefruit knife or spoon.

To make a chrysanthemum flower out of any citrus fruit, cut "teeth" nearly from blossom to stem end (see Figure 6a). Using both hands, gently rotate the fruit and pull it apart (see Figure 6b). Remove pulp for other uses and make sure peel is clean.

FIGURE 2. **Citrus cartwheels in a row, twisted in opposite directions**

Figure 3. Citrus fans made by overlapping half slices. Mint or chocolate leaves are placed on the juncture of the fan.

Figure 4. Staggered scallops of citrus wheels along lines of tray or pan

Figure 5. Coronet or citrus crown placed on scalloped citrus wheel

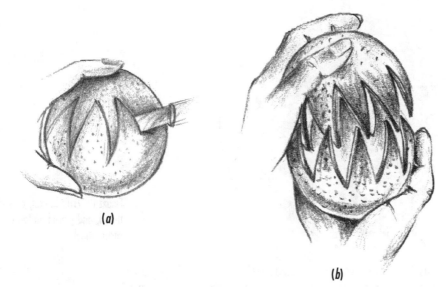

(a)

(b)

FIGURE 6. (a) and (b)
Chrysanthemum, saw-tooth cut
technique

For a vertical garnish, thread chrysanthemum-cut fruits onto a wooden skewer in descending size order (see Figure 7). Perhaps use a kumquat or limequat at the top center. Place skewer on a dish at an angle or break off skewer and surround "flower" with watercress or other greens.

To carve a basket, draw dotted lines on a fruit and use a sharp knife to cut smoothly along them (see Figure 8). Remove the pulp and flute the bottom.

Rind—Peeled, Striped, Curled, Candied

Zested citrus fruits add bright sunshine rays in both appearance and flavor. The stripper can give you a long streak of color, but do not let it overwhelm the dish or palate.

FIGURE 7. Vertical garnish of
skewered citrus fruits

FIGURE 8. Fruit basket, carved, fluted, and placed on larger citrus wheel

For a charming twist, curl back the rind on a citrus half and tie it in a loose knot. Simply peel away the skin almost all the way round, then shape the strip of skin into a bow or knot. Work slightly on a slant, leaving the strip attached at one point (see Figure 9).

To candy citrus peel, boil julienned zest in sugar syrup made of 1 cup sugar, $\frac{1}{2}$ cup water, and $\frac{1}{4}$ cup Grand Marnier or Cointreau. The peel should appear translucent and softened. Drain and cool on rack above wax paper. Save syrup to marinate fruit or to add to fruit drinks.

Apples, Pears, and Peaches

Carving Tools

Peeler for apples, pears, and peaches
Stainless steel kitchen knife

FIGURE 9. Citrus rind peeled back and knotted or tied in a bow

Apple cutter and corer

Fluted pastry cutters ($1\frac{1}{2}$ inches across)

Parisian cutters of various sizes to hollow fruits for stuffing

Scalloped Bases for Fillings

Flute the bottom half of the fruit and dig out the middle. Alternatively, peel and cut the fruit on top and bottom, retaining the center half. Cut the outside with a large fluted cutter and a smaller plain one to cut the core away (see Figure 10).

Hollowed and Poached Fruits

Hollowed and poached fruits may be used as garnishes as well as edible containers. First, poach apples or peaches in fruit juices or sugar syrup until tender. Core the fruit from underneath and hollow out as much space as needed for filling (use any filling you desire). Halve and pit the fruit (see Figure 11).

For almond peaches, add pieces of cinnamon stick and drops of almond oil. Top with toasted nuts.

For brandied apricots or peaches, reduce fruit syrup by half until thickened (about 15 minutes). When cool, add $\frac{1}{4}$ cup brandy and fruit of choice. Refrigerate 2–3 days and serve studded with sliced almonds.

FIGURE 10. Scalloped apple base for fillings and garnishes

FIGURE 11. Hollowed and
poached apples, pears, or peaches

Halved, Sliced, Quartered, Cut into Shapes

Cut and core to any size apple, pear, or peach for service. Halve, slice, or quarter
the fruit or stamp out shapes with cut-outs. Scatter pieces over appropriate dish.
For longer service periods, poach the fruit, rather than using it raw covered in
lemon juice.

Slice and sauté apple rings or pickle, spice, or mull pears or peaches. Scatter
over puddings, custards, or even hot breakfast cereals.

Exotic Fruits

Carving Tools

    Medium-sized knives for peeling and cutting
    Round pastry cutter for coring pineapples
    Parisian cutters, fluted or plain, round or oblong for cutting melon balls
    Fancy waved knives for making decorative trimmings of melon
    Fluter for smaller melons and kiwi

Melon, Pineapple, and Banana Boats, Balls, and Shapes

Flute or cut and scoop out the seeds of melons and papaya or cut and core pineapple.

Sauté pickled or canned pineapple rings or dust fresh pineapple rings with brown sugar and broil briefly. Pickling syrup: $\frac{1}{2}$ cup sugar syrup, $\frac{1}{4}$ cup cider vinegar, 1 teaspoon pickling spice mix. Simmer 10 minutes and strain over pineapple.

Use a baller or Parisian scoop to shape melon balls.

Remove banana flesh after using a sharp, pointed knife to cut away a strip of peel to a depth of about $\frac{1}{8}$ inch, leaving one end attached. Roll the strip back and secure with a toothpick and bright berry, grape, or starfruit. Fill boat with a mixture of small fruits, such as champagne grapes (see Figure 12).

Melon, Papaya, and Kiwi Coronets, Slices, Shapes

Cut through the center of melon or kiwi, zigzag fashion, with a sharp, pointed knife. For a higher back to the coronet, flute with a large or small fluter at an angle instead of dead even in the middle. Remove seeds of melon with a spoon. Fill cavity with bright cherries or grapes of choice and serve on a scalloped grapefruit wheel (see Figures 13a, b, c, d).

Slice or cut shapes with stamps and designs.

Starfruit and Kumquats, Fresh, Preserved in Syrup

Follow procedure for candied orange rind.

For kumquat flowers, use knife or scissors to cut each fruit into six or eight sections. Cut downward three quarters of the way to the bottom so sections will

FIGURE 12. Banana boat with champagne grapes and starfruit topped with a berry garnish

(a)

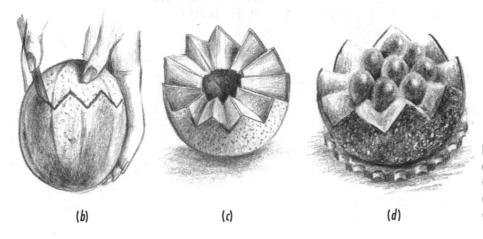

(b)   (c)   (d)

FIGURE 13. (a) Kiwi whole and cut into coronets; (b), (c), and (d) Melon fluted and hollowed out, then filled with grapes or cherries

fan out. Gently spread sections apart and remove a portion of the pulp. Tuck half a candied or minted cherry in the center.

Strawberry Fans, Slices, Crystals

Slice strawberry thinly, just barely to the stem. Gently flare the fan, separating slices (see Figure 14).

Top berries and slice thinly. Decorate at will.

Dip berries by stem into gently simmering sugar syrup or strawberry glaze. Flavor syrup or glaze with Grand Marnier, Cointreau, or other liqueur.

Crystallized Red and Green Grapes

Prepare these several hours ahead and allow them to air dry before using them as garnish around or centered on platters.

For 1 pound of seedless red or green grapes, cut into clusters or fully separate, as desired, whip one egg white and place $\frac{1}{2}$ cup sugar in a shallow bowl. Dip

FIGURE 14. Strawberry fan, sliced and gently flared

grapes into egg white and roll them in sugar. Sprinkle more sugar over grapes as needed until generously coated. Place grapes on a rack and let dry at room temperature for about 3 hours (see Figures 15a, b).

Tubers and Root Vegetables

Carving Tools

 Pastry bag with a variety of tips for piping shapes

 Parisian and other cutters for carrots and celery root, jicama, etc.

 Wavy knives for artistic cutting and trimming

 Saladocca or corkscrew-type cutter for cutting spirals

 Vegetable knives

(a)   (b)

FIGURE 15. (a) and (b) Crystallized red and green grapes, sugared and dried

FIGURE 16. Acorn squash rose
prepared on a slicer

Acorn Squash Rose

Cut squash in half horizontally, and place on professional slicer, and slice $\frac{1}{16}$ to $\frac{1}{8}$ inch thick. Wrap strips around each other, as in a tomato rose, and secure with a toothpick (see Figure 16).

Artichoke Mimosas

Toss cooked quartered artichoke bottoms in French dressing. Into a bowl, sieve hard-cooked eggs (both whites and yolks, or just yolks, can be used) and add about half as much minced parsley. Season to taste with salt and freshly ground white pepper. Dip one edge of each artichoke quarter in the egg mixture. Place like petals of a flower in corner of steam table pan or on edge of serving platter.

Carrot Cut-Out Shapes, Curls, Shreds

Cook carrots or celery root until just softened; slice. Stamp out shapes with star, flower, crescent, or heart cutters. Arrange decoratively. Use stripper or saladocca to create curls or long shreds (see Figure 17).

Fennel Halved, Quartered, Cut Out

Steam or microwave fennel pieces; stamp out shapes of choice. Alternatively, separate layers and halve or quarter for chunks of contrast and crunch.

FIGURE 17. Carrot shapes cut with various stamps

Onion Rings, Coronets, Dice

Slice Spanish onions thinly and brush with egg white if desired (see Figure 18a). Dust with minced violet or chive flowers, gold nasturtiums, or the more familiar parsley and paprika. Flute any color or size onion with fluter or knife and separate (see Figure 18b). Onions may be tinted at will.

Dice red or white onions for color and contrast. Red onions make a less expensive garnish than red bell pepper.

Radish Roses, Blossoms, Water Lilies, Marguerites, Coronets

For the fastest radish rose, press stamp mold into top center of radish and toss into cold water to bloom (see Figure 19a). For a blossom, make four lengthwise and six crosswise incisions, going just beyond the middle of the radish (see Figure 19b). A water lily is more unusual; use a groove knife to cut eight incisions from the top downwards (see Figure 19c). The marguerite requires twelve slashes all around the radish clear to the stalk end. Using the tip of the knife, detach the petals from the white heart, but leave lower ends attached (see Figure 19d). To

(a)

(b)

FIGURE 18. (a) Sliced onion rings; may be brushed with egg white and dusted with minced nasturtiums; (b) Onion fluted to a coronet

make a coronet use the technique described above, but on a tiny scale (see Figure 19e). All root vegetables bloom in cold water for at least an hour or overnight.

Saladocca Spirals and Shreds of Any Root Vegetable

Place elongated chunks of root vegetables in saladocca press. Rotate handle, pressing firmly to achieve long spirals or filaments (see Figure 20). A corkscrew spiral cutter works well on white radishes too.

(a)

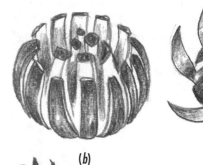

(b)

(c)

(d)

(e)

FIGURE 19. Radish flowers: (a) rose, (b) blossom, (c) water lily, (d) marguerite, (e) coronet.

FIGURE 20. **Saladocca hand machine for spirals, shreds, and thin chips**

Root Vegetable Chrysanthemums, Brushes, and Calla Lilies

Scallions, leeks, carrots, radishes, rutabagas, and turnips may be made into chrysanthemums by slicing repeatedly down their length nearly to the root or bottom.

A trimmed and peeled turnip is most easily held between two chopsticks or wooden spoon handles, which prevents the knife from cutting all the way through. Begin by cutting horizontally to the cutting board in the thinnest possible slices. Turn the turnip ninety degrees and make another series of slices perpendicular to the first. Soak in salted water for about ten minutes or until flower blooms. Rinse well and chill or color at will. Gently move "petals" about to give a more realistic appearance (see Figure 21a). Also try roasting potatoes cut this way next to a roast.

Brushes or dahlias are easily made. Hold a 1- to 3-inch length of scallion in your left hand. Insert a sharp paring knife through the stem at the point you wish the bristles to begin. Draw knife upward, cutting all the way to the tip (see Figure 21b). Carry on, turning the scallion or leek after each cut. If making curls on both ends, be sure to leave at least one quarter-inch unsliced in the middle. Soak veg-

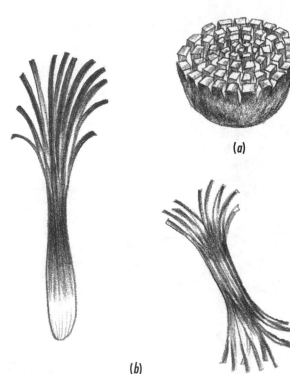

(a)

(b)

Figure 21. (a) Turnip or potato chrysanthemum; (b) Scallion brush and fan

etables in ice water at least one hour, occasionally spreading the petals apart to fluff them up (see Figure 21c).

Use peeled and thinly sliced white or yellow turnips to make calla lilies. Simply wrap slices around baby carrots or ears of corn. These will keep overnight if placed in ice water in the refrigerator. With the addition of scallion greens or leaves of leek, they make a beautiful garnish around a leg of pork or glazed ham for a special spring dinner menu on a steam table or carving board.

To make twelve lilies, you'll need one 8-ounce turnip and twelve baby carrots or corn. Cut the turnip crosswise into paper-thin slices ($\frac{1}{16}$ inch or less) with a meat slicer, very sharp knife, or mandoline. Refer to Figure 22a and wrap one slice of turnip around carrot so that point is upward and the turnip slice overlaps near the base. Hold in place with a toothpick.

Place each lily in ice water as it is completed. When ready to garnish, remove the lilies from the ice bath and snip off most of the toothpick, using poultry shears or wire cutters. Arrange them around meat; use greens cut into pointed shapes between and around the flowers (see Figure 22b).

Squash Flowers

These are actual flowers. Remove them from the squash and clean them gently. They do not last as long as constructed garnishes.

(a)

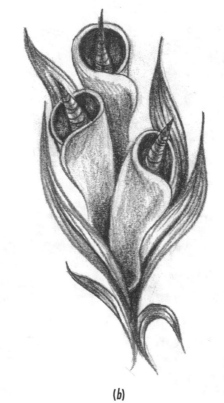

(b)

Figure 22. (a) Calla lily, single flower; (b) Bouquet of calla lilies with leek leaves

Gourds and Cucumbers

Carving Tools

Olive-shaped, round, and elongated Parisian cutters for cucumber and zucchini decorations

Grooving and cutting knives for decorating cucumbers

Larger knives for cutting and decorating pumpkins and large gourds

Cucumber Wedges, Balls, Coronets

English cucumber is best for garnishes because it need not be peeled and has no large seeds. Cut portion desired in half lengthwise, then cut the halves into wedges. Arrange these one behind another, side by side, in a ring, or around a hard-cooked egg (see Figure 23a).

For cucumber balls, peel cucumber if desired; scoop out firm flesh with a Parisian cutter or small melon baller. Arrange in a ring or as a bunch of grapes. Cut the peel into grape-leaf shape (see Figure 23b), or use leek leaves.

(a)

(c)

(b)

FIGURE 23. (a) Cucumber wedges overlapped; (b) Balls arranged as grapes with leaves cut from cucumber peel; (c) Cucumber coronet

The fluted coronet technique works best on 4-inch lengths; the result is a great base for other embellishments (see Figure 23c).

Pickle, Pepper, Cornichon, Chili, and Gherkin Fans

Fans can be made from these vegetables and carrots and zucchini as well. Cut lengths along vegetable from the broad end to the crux of the fan, leaving $1/8$ to $1/4$ inch. Place in cold salted water until the segments open slightly. Gently fan open even more (see Figures 24a, b, c).

Summer Squashes, Sliced, Cut in Shapes

Slice squashes horizontally or vertically. Cut vertical slices with various stamps.

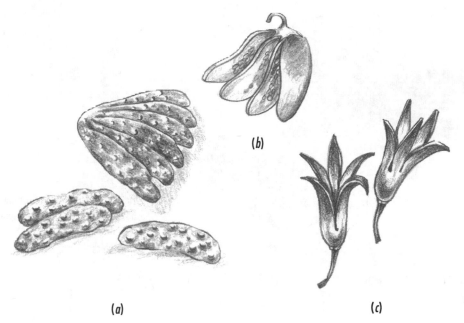

(b)

(a)

(c)

FIGURE 24. (a) and (b) Cornichon pickle and chile fans; (c) Chile flowers

Zucchini Boats, Barges

Hollow out cooked zucchini or yellow squash to make boat (see Figure 25a). Split squash lengthwise and cut halves into 3-inch lengths, then round the ends with a knife (see Figure 25b). Trim undersides for greater stability and hollow with a small scoop. Flute $1\frac{1}{2}$-inch lengths. Fill barges with baby corn, carrots, or whatever suits.

Mushrooms

Carving Tools

    Small vegetable knife and groove knife for turning
    Stripper or grove knife

Grooved, Turned Mushrooms

Draw grooving knife from center of cap downward seven or eight times. Sprinkle with lemon juice.
    Work with shape blade or stripper at an angle between thumb and forefinger. Draw the knife downward from the center of the cap repeatedly, sickle fashion.

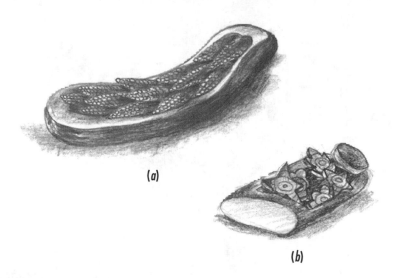

(a)

(b)

FIGURE 25. (*a*) and (*b*) Zucchini boats and barges filled with baby corn and little stamped vegetables

Pull stalk from large mushroom caps and trim and clean. Batter and deep fry if desired (see Figure 26).

Tomatoes and Peppers

Carving Tools

    Cutters in a variety of shapes and sizes

    Knives in a variety of sizes

Halved, Quartered, Sliced

Halve, slice, or quarter a variety of colored bell peppers for rainbow garnishes.

Rings, Julienne, Chiffonade, Dice, Stamps

Slice peppers to rings, julienne, shreds, or dice with French knife. Cut the sides away from stem and bottom of pepper and stamp any shape needed. You can build flowers from crescent, bud, and leaf shapes (see Figure 27).

Baskets, Edible Containers

Cut top away from pepper or tomato and carve a handle. Hollow vegetable with paring knife; flute, carve, or decorate at will. Serve dips or fillings in steamed edible containers (See Figure 28).

FIGURE 26. Grooved, turned, sliced mushrooms

FIGURE 27. Peppers halved and cut to decorative designs

FIGURE 28. Basket or edible container, carved, hollowed, and filled with edible flowers

PASTRY BAG TECHNIQUES

Push the tip forward inside the bag until the point sticks through the hole at the end. Hold the bag in your left hand (if you are right-handed) and fold the top edge down and over your fist.

Fill the bag with whipped cream, crème patissière, or other food to be piped, using a rubber or plastic spatula. Bring the clean edge up above your fist and smooth the filled bag toward the pastry tube tip.

Twist the clean edge around the top of the filled bag. Practice a rosette or scalloped edge on plate or surface other than the dish to be garnished. This also eliminates air bubbles from the bag.

Work straight over your main dish. Use your left hand to exert even pressure on the bag and your right hand to guide the tip. (Of course, 'lefties' should reverse hands.) With a bit of practice, you can make scalloped edges or rounded running circles. The perfect rosette of whipped cream or puréed potatoes may be more difficult to handle. Use puréed vegetables from the color charts in Chapter 1 to add flair to almost any dish.

Paper Cones

Most chefs make their own paper cones for delicate piping and ribbons of chocolate icing. These may be refrigerated with any remaining icing for later use.

Cut your own triangles from parchment, butcher paper, or waxed paper, or buy ready-made triangles at a cake decorating center. With the long edge facing downward, fold two points up to make a triangular cone shape.

Form a rounded cone with the inside and outside edges resting on top of one another. Grasp the cone at the seam with your thumbs outside. Work the thumbs up the paper, drawing the cone tighter until the point of the cone is very sharp and completely closed.

Hold the cone tightly to keep it from unfolding and turn the points inward. Staple it, if desired.

Fill the cone, then turn the sides inward again and fold the top down onto itself once or twice to keep the filling from escaping.

Carefully cut off the tip. Be sure the opening is not too large. For writing, simply cut the top off straight at the size you wish (see Figure 29).

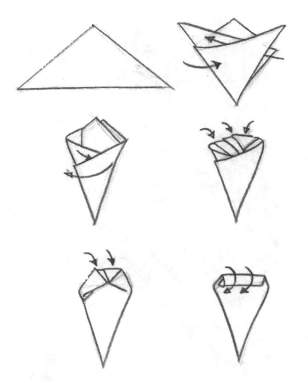

FIGURE 29. Paper cone folding technique

CHOCOLATE WORK

Many white and dark chocolate cups, leaves, and sacks may be purchased. Some even come with rainbows of color or a patina of real gold leaf. Check the cost of purchase against the cost of your labor. It may be worthwhile to save yourself the trouble.

Carving Tools

    Spatula, knives, various small cutters

    Brushes

    Small paper sacks

    Piping bag for thin lines of decorative chocolate

Chocolate Piping, Ribbons, Sacks

Draw a pattern on butcher or white paper with black felt pen. Cover with grease-proof or baking sheet paper. Pour chocolate icing into a waxed-paper cone or

FIGURE 30. Chocolate piping design

small pastry bag. Pipe along design showing through tracing paper (see Figure 30). Leave ornaments to harden. Remove with a sharp knife.

Pipe thicker outlines for ribbons.

Paint a small paper sack with tempered couverture (see Figure 31). Sprinkle with sugar or decorations and let set until hardened but not brittle. Peel away paper sack.

Spread tempered couverture on greaseproof paper on chilled marble or board and leave to harden slightly. Dip stamps in hot water before cutting. Wait until couverture has set harder before breaking designs away. Cutters in traditional shapes are also used for marzipan and aspic jelly.

Select nontoxic leaves of various shapes and sizes, leaving the stem attached. Dip one side of the leaf in melted chocolate that is just slightly cooled. Be sure to coat the leaf well. Let cool, leaf side down, on waxed paper or parchment. For curved leaves, lay coated leaves to cool in a French bread baking pan, leaf side down. Refrigerate ten to fifteen minutes, if the day or room is warm. Carefully peel the leaf off the set chocolate; refrigerate chocolate leaves until needed. Place chocolate leaves on top of desserts such as pie, cake, or chocolate mousse (see Figure 32).

FIGURE 31. Making a chocolate sack

FIGURE 32. Powdered doily art under slice of meringue pie with chocolate leaves fanned on top

POWDERED SUGAR AND COCOA POWDER

Tools

Scissors, parchment paper, rulers, patterns, props
Fine nylon mesh sieves or dredgers, for dusting cakes and plates evenly

Powdered Doilies, Patterns, Latticework

Cut a round of paper slightly larger than your product. Fold in half and half again. Use kitchen shears to cut a design in the sides of the folded circle. When opened, the design should be symmetrical. A doily can be used as well. Or, cut $\frac{1}{2}$-inch-wide strips of paper and weave through each other at an angle to form a lattice. Place pattern gently on dessert or plate and dust with sugar or cocoa. Very carefully lift stencil off; serve dessert when desired (refer to Figure 32).

Silhouettes of Forks, Spoons, Stars, Other Shapes

Tailor the decoration to the occasion. Use the stenciling technique to produce forks, spoons, stars, musical notes, four-leaf clovers, initials, Cupids, etc., on dessert plates.

EQUIPMENT

Essential gourmet gear includes all the tools you need to prepare low-cost, gorgeous, delicious garnishes—fast and fresh. These lists include knives as well as other miscellaneous tools (see Color Plate 2).

High-Quality Knives

At minimum, you'll need:

Paring knife
3-inch turning knife

5–6-inch thin-bladed, full-tang boning knife, best quality

Steak knife

10–12-inch chef's or French knife

Serrated bread knife

All should be made of high-carbon stainless steel, which is easy to sharpen yet resistant to corrosion.

You'll also need a sharpening steel. The longer the steel and the coarser its grooves, the more efficient it is.

Gadgets, Tools, Smallwares

Stripper, zester

Vegetable peelers

Canapé cutters, plain and grooved

Set of pastry and Parisian cutters, fluted and plain

Radish rose stamps

Other stamps and cutters of choice (e.g., shaped like animals, leaves, trees, hearts, and flowers)

Spiral slicer

Wavy knives

Serrated fruit knife with curved end

Corrugated garnishing knife

Apple wedger and corer

Birds' nest fryer

Melon ballers, various sizes and shapes

Ice cream scoops, various sizes

Fluters, various sizes

Sketching tools

V- and *U*-shaped chisels

Brushes of various sizes and shapes, at least some with natural bristles

Sauce whisks

Slotted spoons

Small bottle tongs and large serrated cooking tongs

Short- and long-handled two-tined utility forks

Heavy-duty soup and sauce ladles, various sizes

Saladocca or oriental shredder

Mandoline

Mouli grater

Fine nylon mesh sieves

Piping bags and tips of various sizes and shapes

Wide-bladed, flat metal and plastic spatulas

6–9-inch narrow-bladed, flat metal spatula or palette knife

Butter molds and curlers

Hard-cooked-egg slicer

Tomato wedger

Dredger for cocoa and powdered sugar

Small graters for ginger and nutmeg

Salad spinner

Citrus juicer or reamer

Set of skewers and used dental tools

Parchment paper and cheesecloth

Kitchen twine

Kitchen shears

Fancy muffin and cookie tins

Brioche, dariole, bombe, and charlotte molds

Copper beating bowl

Mortar and pestle

Hand-held and heavy-duty electric mixers

DELI TRAYS
AND PLATTERS

3

Is it possible to find creative alternatives to the round black plastic trays in your grocery, deli, or catering firm? Here are some easy and inexpensive ideas for improving the platters and adding to the prop closet. Fortunately, creative arrangements and garnishes can overcome banality in the tray itself. The tray can be a mere backdrop or canvas for your good food arranging.

*Published by Crown Publishing, Inc., © 1988.

If time allows for personal propping, search garage sales and secondhand and consignment stores for odd pieces, clean and use your own mirrors, or pick up unique trays at thrift shops. Fabric stores almost give away small swatches; surround your trays with these for color and texture or use as a background.

Continue the theme of your party with other props and centerpieces. Keep in mind the occasion, season, mood, and motif. Send out rustic breads in a basket rather than a flat tray. Fling a few colorful, edible flowers across your platter for a festive touch. Tuck in a small bouquet of flowering herbs as a thoughtful gesture to the hostess.

Usually, though, deli platters go out on their own. Develop a signature tray arrangement; try for anything rather than rolled meats and shingled cheese slices.

As suggested in Chapter 2, consider asking customers to supply their own trays. Alternatively, ask for a deposit or place your arrangement on a heavy piece of marble they won't want to keep.

During peak or rush periods, trays need to go out quickly. Meet your deadlines, but do take a moment to garnish. Chapter 1 describes adornments that take but a brief moment and a trifling additional sum. Each 16–18-inch platter should take only thirty minutes to prepare. A 12-inch tray usually serves five to ten, a 16-inch tray serves ten to twenty, and an 18-inch tray serves twenty to thirty.

The following classic deli platters are a starting point on which to base new arrangements and food flows. They are simply a springboard for your own creativity. Make the time to be flexible and to enjoy good food fun.

Sketch your arrangement or play with ideas first. Use architectural graph paper for scaling your concept to size. Obtain color chips from a local paint store to detail the exact hues you desire.

Large blocks of white and yellow cheeses are great for framing elements when placed in the corners of a serving tray or platter. Of course, fanning the contrasting cheeses in a curvaceous flow adds eye appeal, particularly when good rustic breads are available. With an eye to visual elegance and whimsical garnishes, such as a lemon basket stuffed with flowering herbs, you can send out your platters with pride (see Color Plate 3).

COLD MEATS AND CHEESES

Build your tray for visual enhancement. Retain some larger chunks of cheeses and whole meats on the bone. Layer or fan the slices in a flow away from the original source in a graceful manner. If a retro-1950s look is appropriate cube the meats and cheeses.

Cheese and Meat Tray

See Color Plate 4 for a starting point for a staggered arrangement.

YIELD: 20–25 servings

INGREDIENTS

1 pound Tillamook, longhorn, or any other high-quality cheese

1 pound Swiss, pepperjack, or Gouda-style cheese

$1^1/_2$ pounds sliced roasted or smoked turkey

$1^1/_2$ pounds high-quality ham

$1^1/_2$ pounds roast or corned beef

MATERIALS AND GARNISHES

Edible container *or* 6-inch bowl

$^1/_2$ pound kalamata olives

$^1/_2$ pound cornichons

Lengthwise slices of dill pickles (as needed)

1 small bunch ornamental purple kale or green leaf

Golden and red cherry or pear tomatoes

Frilled toothpicks

INSTRUCTIONS

Assemble all ingredients and materials before starting. Fan triangles and cheese slices according to photo. Shape slices of roast beef, ham, turkey, and beef into roses, ruffles, swirls, or *S*-folds and place on platter. Ornament with purple kale.

Fill center of container bowl with olives and cornichons. Fold pickles around edge of edible container. Cut additional leaves of kale in half along vein and place around bowl and between meat slices. Place tomatoes on frilled toothpicks and set on kale. *Note:* For smaller trays, use 1 ounce of each meat per person.

✳ COLD CUT PLATTER

Sometimes the most popular item is that which the guests have the most difficulty identifying. Plan a few surprises for these experimental eaters with flavored seitan, lower-fat meats, tofu pups, or smoked meats or sausages.

YIELD: 20–25 servings

INGREDIENTS

$1^1/_2$ pounds cotto salami, sandwich sliced

$1^1/_2$ pounds turkey ham, sandwich sliced

$1^1/_2$ pounds bologna or seitan, sandwich sliced or cut to fingers

$1^1/_2$ pounds pepper loaf, sandwich sliced, or $1^1/_2$ pounds chicken or turkey sausages, grilled and sliced lengthwise

MATERIALS AND GARNISHES

California ripe olives, as desired

1 pound bread-and-butter pickle chips or cornichons

4 golden cherry tomatoes

1 bunch ornamental purple kale

18-inch round tray and dome lid

6-inch decorative bowl, edible or not

INSTRUCTIONS

Assemble all ingredients and materials before starting. Place pickles and olives in bowl and set in center of tray. Fold each slice of meat into an *S*, cornucopia, or roll and place on tray around bowl in layers, as shown in Color Plate 4. Use lengthwise-sliced sausages to separate contrasting meats.

Place kale around bowl. Stab cherry tomatoes with frilled picks and set on kale.

Optional garnishes: stripes of kalamata olives between meats, bell pepper or red onion rings, marinated fennel, cups of raddichio filled with small olives, crumbled feta, sunflower, sprouts

CHICKEN CITRUS TENDERS, WINGS OF FIRE, AND DIABLO DRUMMETTES WITH DIPPING SAUCES

Chicken breast strips, tenders, wings, or drummettes may be marinated in almost any mixture, then beer-battered, fried, and sauced, or simply breaded and baked (see Color Plate 5). Serve on heated marble slabs.

Do try dipping sauces other than the ubiquitous teriyaki, barbecue, and ranch dressing. If you think these sauces are desired or expected by guests, at least add a twist—serve three-citrus teriyaki, southwest barbecue, or fat-free rosemary lemon saffron sauce.

YIELD: 10–12 servings

INGREDIENTS

5–6 pounds chicken tenders

5–6 pounds chicken wings or small chicken drumsticks (drummettes)

$1^1/_2$ cups Lemon-Lime Tequila Sauce (see below)

3 tablespoons coarse sea salt

3 tablespoons paprika

3 tablespoons lemon pepper

3 medium red onions, minced, or 3 tablespoons onion powder

3 tablespoons red pepper flakes, heaping if desired

1 tablespoon garlic

1 tablespoon chili powder

$1^1/_2$ teaspoons cumin

$1^1/_2$ pints high-quality barbecue sauce

LEMON LIME TEQUILA SAUCE

$^2/_3$ cup lemon juice

$^2/_3$ cup tequila

2 tablespoons fresh basil, chopped

2 tablespoons fresh rosemary, chopped

2 cloves garlic, minced

2 teaspoons lime zest

INSTRUCTIONS
CHICKEN CITRUS TENDERS

Marinate tenders in Lemon-Lime Tequila Sauce for at least 1 hour. Bread, if desired, and simply grill, sauté, bake, or broil.

(Continued)

LEMON-LIME TEQUILA SAUCE

Combine all ingredients.

WINGS OF FIRE AND DIABLO DRUMMETTES

Preheat oven to 400°F. Divide wings and drummettes among hotel pans. Mix all spices with barbecue sauce. Pour two thirds of the sauce over wings and drummettes, saving the rest for a dipping sauce. Bake for 20 minutes.

Serve with celery and carrot sticks and Rosemary Lemon Saffron Sauce, blue cheese, or Southwest Barbecue Dipping Sauce.

* ROSEMARY LEMON SAFFRON SAUCE

Mix desired amounts of lemon zest, juice, minced rosemary, and saffron or turmeric with nonfat quark or cream cheese and sour cream or plain yogurt.

* SOUTHWEST BARBECUE DIPPING SAUCE

Combine 1 pint high-quality barbecue sauce with 1 teaspoon red pepper flakes, 1 teaspoon crushed garlic, 1 teaspoon chili powder, 1 teaspoon cumin, 1 teaspoon cinnamon, 2 teaspoons lime juice, $^{1}/_{4}$ cup cilantro leaves, and $^{1}/_{4}$ cup or 2 ounces of minced red or green onion.

SOUTHWESTERN SEASONING/BREADING

If you can possibly retreat from frozen breaded chicken tenders and strips, try this food formula and see how fast and fresh it is. This is like a Southwestern shake and bake. Toss slices or chunks of aging bread in the freezer. When the quantity builds up, defrost the bread and process it in the food processor or buffalo chopper. Croutons are easy, too, and much better when mixed with your own pure blend of seasonings.

YIELD: Enough to coat 12 servings of chicken tenders

INGREDIENTS

2 cups yellow, white, or blue cornmeal

1 cup dry unseasoned breadcrumbs

$^3/_4$ cup Romano, asiago, or Parmesan cheese, freshly grated

3 tablespoons chili powder

3 tablespoons ground cumin

2 tablespoons ground cloves

2 tablespoons cinnamon

2 tablespoons red pepper flakes

1 tablespoon sugar

Egg whites, as needed

INSTRUCTIONS

Preheat oven to 400°F. Combine all ingredients except egg whites in a large zippered plastic bag and shake. Lightly whip whites and pour into a shallow dish. Dip poultry pieces in egg white; turn each to coat. Put chicken in bag, seal, and shake. Place in half or full hotel pan sprayed with Baker's Release or olive oil spray. Lightly coat chicken with spray. Bake for 15–30 minutes or until done.

THREE-CITRUS TERIYAKI SAUCE

This recipe was first developed for a fast-food chicken chain. It appeared later in a seafood magazine and then was used in an Italian panini restaurant and at many a party. It is superb with both chicken and fish as either a marinade or a dipping sauce.

YIELD: 56 ounces

(Continued)

INGREDIENTS

1 pint light soy, shoyu, or Dr. Bragg's sauce

1^1/$_2$ pints white wine (chablis)

1 cup Amontillado dry sherry

1 ounce lemon juice

1 ounce orange juice

1 ounce lime juice

2 tablespoons ginger, freshly grated

1–2 ounces brown sugar or honey

1 tablespoon garlic, minced

2 tablespoons cornstarch

^{1}/$_2$ cup water

INSTRUCTIONS

Combine soy sauce, white wine, sherry, lemon, orange, and lime juices, ginger, brown sugar, and garlic to make the teriyaki marinade. Pour one half of marinade over chicken and marinate at least 1 hour. Bring remaining teriyaki marinade to a gentle boil in a stockpot. Blend the cornstarch well with the water. Add this mixture to the boiling marinade to thicken. Stir until teriyaki sauce returns to boil and thickens.

Place teriyaki sauce in steam table and serve with chicken in 2-ounce soufflé cups or plastic side cups.

ORIENTAL PLATTERS OF SUSHI, POTSTICKERS, AND EGG ROLLS

At least there has been movement toward a new genre of deli platters featuring Asian cuisine. Showcase sushi, barbecued pork, potstickers, wontons, and miniature egg rolls, which are easy to put out if you get into the rhythm of rolling and wrapping. High-quality frozen products are another easy approach. Serve with chopsticks from a black lacquer octangular tray with little lacquered boxes for additional rice or garnishes; scallion fans are an attractive garnish choice (see Color Plate 6).

Sweet-and-sour, hot mustard, three-citrus teriyaki, and simply seasoned soy are classic dipping sauces.

SWEET-AND-SOUR SAUCE

This was developed in the early 1980s at Del Monte, where I was a food service specialist.

YIELD: $1^1/_4$ cup

INGREDIENTS

8 ounces fresh or canned pineapple, puréed

1 tablespoon soy sauce

1 tablespoon brown sugar

1 tablespoon vinegar

1–2 garlic cloves, minced or pressed

$^1/_4$ teaspoon ground ginger

1 tablespoon cornstarch

1 tablespoon water

GARNISHES

Scallion, thinly sliced on the diagonal
or
Diced green peppers

INSTRUCTIONS

In a small saucepan, combine pineapple purée, soy sauce, brown sugar, vinegar, garlic, and ground ginger. Bring to a boil; reduce heat. Simmer for 10 minutes. Dissolve cornstarch in water. Stir mixture into sauce. Cook, stirring constantly, until sauce thickens. Sprinkle scallion or peppers on top.

HOT GINGERED MUSTARD

Mix hot yellow mustard with wasabi and chopped pickled ginger. Garnish with black and white sesame seeds.

✳ SIMPLE SOY DIPPING SAUCE

Combine light soy sauce with brown sugar, minced fresh ginger and garlic, and a splash of sherry to taste.

SALAD SAMPLERS

Samplers are a platform from which to launch distinctive, low-cost, simple salads of all sorts. A series of grain salads was created for a soup and salad restaurant chain that takes only 35–40 minutes to prepare. While the grains or beans are simmering, the other salad ingredients and the dressing or marinade are prepped.

Many grains are available for experimentation: triticale, hard and soft wheat berries, kashi, spelt, quinoa, and more. These ancient foods are inexpensive, and steam table and salad bar sturdy. They are nutty, hearty, and have a pleasant texture and mouth feel. Each grain has a fascinating history. Spelt, for example, is considered the biblical manna from heaven. Mix in vegetables or fruits and nuts of choice with your favorite dressing or marinade.

The range of bean and lentil varieties is expanding. Take advantage of the many colors and sizes available today. Get to know the subtle taste and texture differences among these healthy legumes.

Molded salads are popular again—macaroni salad, dripping in mayonnaise, is out. Continuous dressing seepage checks are an important quality control measure for deli display cases and salad bars. More salad concepts, dressings, and marinades are covered in Chapter 4.

Serve sampler platters on different levels of marble or Corian with smaller jagged chunks of marble or tile on a pedestal. Grains may be molded into pyramids and timbales. Place dressings and garnishes in smaller edible receptacles or diminutive bowls. (See Color Plate 7.)

Dilled Salmon or Tuna and Kashi: High-fiber kashi unites with a colorful vegetable medley, and dill is the natural fresh herb to pair with each. Nuts add a satisfying textural crunch.

Wild Waldorf Salad: Great for summer patio dining. Add a bit of wild rice and a bit more of brown basmati rice to the traditional Waldorf mixture. For a more substantial salad, mix in chunks of salmon, tuna, smoked turkey cubes, or chicken strips.

Southwest Black Bean Salad: The color, zest, and verve of the Southwest is here. Combine beans with diced roasted bell pepper of every color, chayote, and traditional spices. Try a Brazilian variation with rices too, like a black bean salad-soup.

Bulgur Spring Salad: Mix bulgur with a mix of vegetables, especially artichokes, and almonds. Marinate in a mustard sauce.

Golden Lemon Lentil Salad with Fresh Mint: New yellow and orange lentils present a pastel finish. Combine with carrots, onion, and celery in a lemon mint dressing.

Escarole and White Bean Salad with Fennel and Fontina Cheese: A hearty seasonal salad for winter and early spring. All the prep can be done while the beans are cooking.

Barley Vegetable Salad with Creamy Dilled Dressing: Rice salads abound; barley is more unusual and adds high fiber along with a nutty flavor. This would be a smart make-ahead meal.

Lentil Salad with Oil-free Tarragon Dressing and Vegetable Brunoise: A Greek salad featuring vegetables, feta cheese, and sliced ripe olives.

Creamy Fruity Spelt Tabouli: This grain salad combines dried fruits and nuts with the piquant finish of oranges and a lemony spiced sauce. It is similar to an ambrosia or sweet dessert salad and would be great layered in a parfait glass.

✱ GOLDEN LEMON LENTIL SALAD WITH LEMON MINT DRESSING

Many varieties of lentils are grown in the Palouse areas of Idaho and Washington. Here are two of the most colorful.

YIELD: 8–10 servings

(Continued)

INGREDIENTS

GOLDEN LENTILS

1 pound yellow lentils
1 pound orange lentils
1 quarts cold water
1 bay leaf

3 ounces carrots, diced
3 ounces red onion, diced
3 ounces celery, diced

LEMON MINT DRESSING

$^1/_4$ cup fresh mint, chopped
$^1/_4$ cup fresh parsley, chopped
$^1/_4$ cup fresh cilantro, chopped
1 tablespoon fresh thyme leaves
1 tablespoon lemon zest

Juice of 2 large lemons
$^1/_2$ teaspoon red pepper flakes
$^1/_2$ teaspoon paprika
1 large clove garlic, minced
$^1/_2$ cup safflower or canola oil

GARNISH

Chunks of feta
Lemon wheels

Sprigs of fresh mint

INSTRUCTIONS

GOLDEN LENTILS

Cover lentils with water. Add bay leaf, bring to a boil, cover, and simmer 20–30 minutes. Add diced vegetables in last 5 minutes. Drain.

LEMON MINT DRESSING

Combine all ingredients, whisking oil in slowly. Pour over cooked lentils. Toss garnishes over salad.

PÂTÉS

Most pâtés are best purchased rather than prepared from scratch, which is usually neither labor- nor cost-effective without a Robot Coupe food processor. Do showcase the beautiful layered vegetable pâté options as well as country terrines and chicken liver pâtés. Here is one quite simple pâté, as a reference, that was a great success at many catered affairs and in my cookbook *Entertaining Fast and Fresh.**

Again, the presentation is the key. Cut a few slices of pâté and fan them in front of the loaf. Traditional accompaniments included cornichons (small sour French pickles), thinly sliced crusty baguettes, and Pommery mustard. This is an opportunity to display your own line of mustards, flavored with herbs, citrus fruits, and pomegranate seeds for extra flavor.

✱ CHICKEN LIVER PÂTÉ WITH ARMAGNAC

Many guests who think they don't like chicken livers will find this delicious on rustic baguettes with good country mustard and cornichons. Could it also be the butter, herbs, red wine, or Armagnac that is so good to the livers?

YIELD: 16 servings

INGREDIENTS

2 cups plus $^1/_2$ cup butter

2 pounds chicken livers, halved

$^1/_2$ pound chanterelle, shiitake, portobello, crimini, and button mushrooms in any combination, chopped

$^1/_2$ cup parsley, chopped

$^1/_2$ cup shallots, chopped

1 teaspoon dried thyme

1 teaspoon dried basil

$^1/_3$ cup Armagnac, Cognac, or Madeira

1 cup dry red wine

2 cans ($^3/_7$ ounce) black truffles or 4 ounces chopped pistachios or $^1/_3$ cup green peppercorns (optional)

(Continued)

*Thomas Nelson Publishers, © 1985.

INSTRUCTIONS

Melt $^1/_2$ cup butter over medium-high heat in a wide frying pan. Add chicken livers, mushrooms, parsley, shallots, thyme, and basil and sauté, stirring often, until livers are just firm but slightly pink in the center.

In a small frying pan, warm Armagnac and flambé. Add to livers and shake until flame dies. Add wine, heat to simmering, then let mixture cool to room temperature. Process or blend entire mixture. Add 2 cups butter in chunks, blending until smooth. Fold in optional truffles, pistachios, or green peppercorns.

Pour mixture into two deep 4- to 5-cup loaf pans. Cover and chill overnight. Serve with pâté knife.

Note: Pâté can be prepared one week in advance. Cover and refrigerate until serving time.

SPREADS AND DIPS

Spreads and dips can be featured as dressings on a tray or with lavosh, wraps, or sandwiches. Building bold flavors to carry the break, filling, meats, and cheeses is important. Here are fast and fresh spreads that can be easily thinned to dips or dressings.

★ BOURSIN CREAM

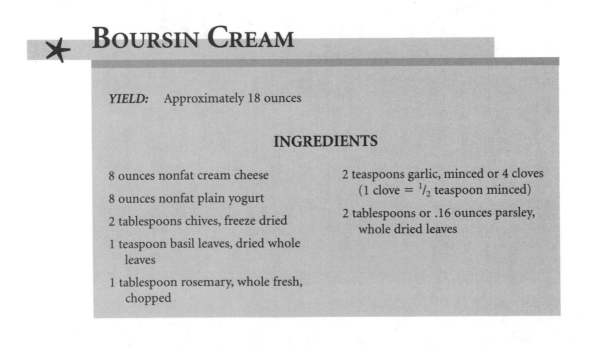

YIELD: Approximately 18 ounces

INGREDIENTS

8 ounces nonfat cream cheese

8 ounces nonfat plain yogurt

2 tablespoons chives, freeze dried

1 teaspoon basil leaves, dried whole leaves

1 tablespoon rosemary, whole fresh, chopped

2 teaspoons garlic, minced or 4 cloves (1 clove = $^1/_2$ teaspoon minced)

2 tablespoons or .16 ounces parsley, whole dried leaves

INSTRUCTIONS

Blend all ingredients and store in covered, dated container.

Note: Boursin cream can be thinned with buttermilk or nonfat evaporated skim milk to make a dressing or dip.

SPARKLING ROASTED RED PEPPER PURÉE

This is superb as a spread or sauce over many foods.

YIELD: $1^3/_4$–2 cups

INGREDIENTS

3 red bell peppers (about 12 ounces), seeded and sliced

4 ounces nonfat cream cheese or quark

2 tablespoons balsamic or raspberry vinegar

1 teaspoon bottled roasted purée of garlic

2 tablespoons thick, hot, chunky salsa, drained

1 tablespoon sugar

$^1/_2$ teaspoon red pepper flakes

INSTRUCTIONS

Place large pieces of red pepper on roasting pan and send through pizza oven or hot convection oven at 450°F for 6 minutes. Process all ingredients with roasted peppers by pulsing blender on and off briefly to produce a thick and chunky spread. Store in a covered, dated container.

Coat meat, fish, or fowl; toss in pasta; spread on bread or use as a dip for most appetizers.

✱ LEMON-LIME AIOLI

YIELD: 3 3/4–4 cups

INGREDIENTS

3 cups light or handmade mayonnaise

3 large garlic cloves, minced

$^1/_4$ cup Asiago, grated

$^1/_2$ cup extra virgin olive oil

Zest of lemon

Zest of lime

1 teaspoon lemon juice

1 teaspoon lime juice

$^1/_4$–$^1/_2$ teaspoon red pepper flakes

Salt and freshly ground black pepper
   to taste

INSTRUCTIONS

Mix all ingredients in large bowl. Refrigerate in a covered, dated container.

✱ PEPPERCORN PARMESAN DIP/SPREAD

Blend 1 tablespoon crushed black peppercorns and 1 tablespoon crushed green peppercorns with 8 ounces cream cheese, 2 ounces Parmesan, freshly grated, 1 ounce buttermilk, and $^1/_2$ teaspoon salt. Refrigerate in covered, dated container.

✱ CREAMY HORSERADISH HONEY MUSTARD

Blend 8 ounces nonfat cream cheese, 8 ounces creamed horseradish, and 8 ounces Inglehoff honey mustard. Refrigerate in covered, dated container.

INTERNATIONAL CHEESE AND FRUIT TASTING

Cheese tasting need not be limited to fruits. A few toasted nuts, such as filberts, almonds, and walnuts, and a scattering of various olives are a beautiful and flavorful addition. Italian or domestic prosciutto, Spanish serrano ham, or any well-cured meat should be sliced paper thin. Dried fruits, such as dates, figs, cherries, and cranberries, and chutneys, as well as the freshest, most aromatic fruits available make for a still life masterpiece (see Color Plate 8).

If possible, serve rustic peasant loaves of bread with a crusty, crunchy crust, whether whole wheat, sourdough, olive bread, or baguettes. These breads are slightly more expensive and much more presentable, tasteful, and showy. They give your guests the impression that you care about quality.

Crostini alone in an upright container add height as an edible centerpiece or prop. Make sure cheese boards and plates are level and provide a sharp, sturdy little knife for each cheese. Dental floss is great for sectioning soft fresh cheeses (as well as softer pâtés), such as chèvre, ahead of service.

Here is a balanced option for the marble, granite, or Corian cheese board. Present a spectrum of types and textures of cheeses from one country. Vary the milk base—use goat-, sheep-, and cowmilk cheeses—and present hard, soft, and semisoft, fresh and aged cheeses.

Identify each cheese on a little placard with its name, type, origin, and manufacturer and a short description of its flavor and strength. You might also note what type of wine it goes best with.

Below is a list of cheeses to use as a starting point and resource list. Of course, whatever cheeses you choose, bring them to room temperature before serving. Keep strong cheeses separate from each other so aromas do not intermingle and generate a confusion of flavors. Grape leaves, paper cheese leaves, straw, and raffia make a nice base for the presentation.

Cheese List for Choice Selections

France

Camembert

Chaumes

Chèvre, regular, flavored, and nonfat

Daux de Montagne

Gourmandise with Kirsch and walnut

Langres or Laguiole

Port-Salut or Esrom

Saint André or Saint Marcellin from Dauphine, France

Switzerland

Baby Swiss round or domestic Emmentaler

Swiss Gruyère

England

Heart of England

Huntsman (layered Gloucester and Stilton)

Red Leicester or farmhouse Cheshire

Stilton

Italy

Asiago, shaved

Fontina Val d'Aosta

Fresh buffalo mozzarella balls

Canada

Black Diamond white Cheddar

United States

Maytag Bleu

Sally Jackson's sheep cheese

White Cheddar of your choice

Mix and match foods and regional wines to bring out the nuances of each flavor and how they interact.

ANTIPASTI AND MARINATED VEGETABLES

When serving antipasti, do use high-quality, fresh items rather than the contents of bottles and cans, full of brine and artificial chemical wash. Marinate vegetables, meats, and salads in your own mixtures. So many antipasti are often dripping in oil, if not brine. Lighten them with a light bath of marinade and serve the rest of the dressing separately.

Here is a variation of a successful food formula developed for a popular Seattle soup and salad bar. The FATT is as follows:

Flavor: vibrant, refreshing herb vinaigrette flavors

Appearance: bright color contrasts among ingredients

Temperature: chilled, 40–50°F

Texture: varied textures and al dente vegetables

ANTIPASTO CHOP-CHOP SALAD

YIELD: 3 lbs (yield of dressing alone is $5^1/_2$ oz.)

INGREDIENTS
DRY SALAD MIX

4 ounces bay shrimp, peeled, deveined, and cooked

3 ounces cucumber, quartered lengthwise and sliced into $^1/_2$-inch pieces

3 ounces fontina, diced into $^1/_4$-inch cubes

1 ounce red onion, peeled and diced into $^1/_4$-inch cubes

3 ounces dry salami, sliced into $^1/_4$-inch slices and quartered

4 ounces garbanzo beans, drained

1 ounce kalamata olives, pitted and coarsely chopped

6 ounces broccoflower florets, blanched al dente

4 ounces carrots, peeled and julienned into $^1/_8$-inch pieces

2 ounces yellow or green bell peppers, cored and diced into $^1/_2$-inch cubes

2 ounces red bell peppers, cored and diced into $^1/_2$-inch cubes and roasted, if time permits

4 ounces frozen cut green beans, drained, or celery cut into 1-inch diagonal chunks

DRESSING

2 fluid ounces canola or safflower oil

2 fluid ounces balsamic vinegar

1 fluid ounce red wine vinegar

1 fluid ounce lemon juice

$^1/_2$ teaspoon steak or sea salt

1 teaspoon whole dried Italian or French herb blend

1 tablespoon Dijon or Pommery mustard

$^1/_4$–$^1/_2$ teaspoon garlic, roasted purée or minced

$^1/_8$–$^1/_4$ teaspoon crushed red pepper

INSTRUCTIONS
DRESSING

Whisk together all the ingredients except the oil in a small bowl. Slowly whisk in oil and blend until dressing emulsifies. Reserve.

(Continued)

SALAD

Toss the dry salad mix ingredients. Add the reserved dressing and toss to coat salad. Serve on a chiffonade bed of savoy or napa cabbage; mix cabbage with chopped romaine if available. (See Color Plate 7 for final dish.)

Vegetable Trays

Make your own magnificent marinade to add a fresh touch to vegetable dishes. Raw crudités are dull; the color is much brighter when the vegetables are steamed briefly. Bathed in a marinade of bold flavors, the crudités will shine in appearance and taste.

When arranging your tray, try a checkerboard of colors rather than a fan of foods emanating from the center, or angle sectors diagonally across the tray. Scattering colors and shapes would lend a free wheeling nonchalance to your arrangement.

This first marinade could be great as a salad dressing for greens, pasta, or potato salad or as a marinade for fish.

This second memorable marinade is superb over grilled vegetables, a favorite for vegetarians and healthy eaters. If you have access to a wood-fired oven or the time and place to grill these marinated vegetables, your platter will rise to a new level of taste and sale price! Bestow on your guests a rainbow of color—golden pear or cherry tomatoes, green, yellow, and red bell peppers, portobello mushrooms, and squashes of various hues, including chayote.

⋆ MAGNIFICENT MARINADE

Mix $^1/_2$ cup lemon juice and $^1/_2$ cup orange juice with grated zest of 2 oranges, $^1/_2$ cup fresh mint, chopped, $^1/_2$ cup fresh cilantro, chopped, 4 cloves garlic, minced, 4 jalapeños, seeded and chopped, 2 teaspoons ground cumin, 2 teaspoons coriander, 1 teaspoon paprika, and $1^1/_3$ cups olive oil.

⭐ MEMORABLE MARINADE

Mix 4–6 green onions, sliced, 1 Scotch bonnet or habanero chili, seeded, stemmed, and minced, $^1/_2$ cup light soy sauce or Dr. Bragg's amino acids, $^1/_2$ cup malt or red wine vinegar, 3 tablespoons lime or lemon juice, 3 tablespoons walnut oil or any vegetable oil, 1 tablespoon fresh oregano, chopped, 1 tablespoon fresh thyme, chopped, $^1/_2$ teaspoon cinnamon, $^1/_2$ teaspoon ground nutmeg, $^1/_4$ teaspoon ground cloves, $^1/_4$ teaspoon cumin, and $^1/_4$ teaspoon allspice.

BREAD TRAYS, ROLLED WRAPS, AND LAVOSH

Develop a relationship with a local baker of peasant breads, whether Italian, French, or any other speciality. Just as in restaurants, breads make the first impression on diners. Wrap flavored breads in colorful cloth and lay them gently in a rustic basket.

Even if nothing but white, wheat, and rye bread slices are in your inventory, a bright patterned or colored paper or cloth napkin frames the bread nicely. Cut slices with a large spade, heart, or flower stamp and toast plain. Spread with flavored butters or roasted pepper purée for greater taste. Cut off crusts or stamp out designs. Bake or toast under the salamander for a flavorful variation and prettier presentation (see Color Plate 9).

I witnessed an opulent still life buffet at the Breakers Hotel in Florida. In a large, elegant banquet room, a gold-sprayed tree of willow limbs was displayed at an angle to the long banquet table. Small bagels and crusty rolls were impaled on the branches to be picked at will from the tree of bread and life. This was a bit of a departure from the usual breadbaskets.

For simpler affairs, make sure there is a variety of crusty peasant breads, however they are served. Seemingly, every town these days has at least one good Italian or rustic-style baker, and focaccia, rosemary, and olive breads are delicious. Your customers should appreciate the richer and denser breads and be willing to pay for them.

When serving wraps or lavosh, experiment with the new colored tortillas of sundried tomatoes, pesto, and pepper rainbows. Chapati, nan, pita, Sardinian cracker bread, and whole-wheat tortillas are other options. Remember, the spreads on these breads should be bold in flavor as well as color, if possible.

Compound butters are another bright and tasty option for wraps and breads. Papaya Citrus Butter, Honey Lime Butter, and Fiesta Butter are but a few of the

✳ DRIED CRANBERRY PESTO

This is an example developed for an Italian bistro. It goes well on Italian filone or a baguette with smoked turkey or grilled chicken breast, rolled up with fillings in lavosh. Purée or process until semi-chunky or smooth: 2 cups dried cranberries, 3 large garlic cloves, 1 ounce thawed raspberries, 3 tablespoons whole-grain mustard, and 3 tablespoons parsley.

✳ JALAPEÑO AVOCADO MAYONNAISE

Purée desired amounts of jalapeño, avocado, and mayonnaise for a bright spring-green spread. Vary with cilantro and lime juice and zest or green chili mayonnaise.

blends I developed for a Seattle-based seafood magazine and a Mexican restaurant chain in Ohio, years ago. The fat, cost, and cholesterol may be reduced by cutting the butter with nonfat quark or nonfat cream cheese.

Bread and roll trays should price out (at least on the West Coast) at around $10.00 for 12-inch trays serving 15–25, $20.00 for 16-inch trays serving 25–40, and $30.00 for 18-inch trays serving 40–55 guests. Make sure your condiment tray is creative and varied and features signature mustards, mayonnaise, butter blends, and spreads in dainty, singular containers.

An aram or lavosh tray could showcase vegetarian and meat fillings. A 12-inch tray might serve 8–12 and a 16-inch tray 12–25. The hunger of the crowd is always an unknown factor.

Mini-sandwich trays may be a profit center in the afternoon. Recommend or sell English and herbal teas with traditional tea sandwiches and a few that you developed on your own.

Consider a calligraphic quote about how tea is sweetened best by love and scandal. This will add to an ambience of artistry and eccentricity. You won't be forgotten for the next catered party or to-go deli tray.

✱ PAPAYA CITRUS BUTTER

Where papaya or mango is used, this citrus butter has a taste of summer that melts over breads, fish, poultry—and in the mouth.

YIELD: 8 servings

INGREDIENTS

1 cup unsalted butter or $1/2$ cup unsalted butter and $1/2$ cup quark

2 medium papayas, peeled, seeded and cubed (about 1 cup)

$1/3$ cup Amontillado sherry or Champagne or Chardonnay

1 tablespoon plus 1 teaspoon lime juice

1 tablespoon plus 1 teaspoon orange juice

2 teaspoons honey

1 teaspoon lime zest, grated

1 teaspoon orange zest, grated

INSTRUCTIONS

In a small saucepan over medium heat, melt butter or butter and quark. Add papaya; simmer until softened, 4–5 minutes. Blend or process with remaining ingredients until smooth.

COOKIE, DESSERT, AND PASTRY PLATTERS

Ah, the grand finale! Make sure your dessert fare offers indulgent and moderate choices, including fresh seasonal fruits and lower-fat spa cuisine choices. Molded desserts such as a creamy apricot mousse or Pineapple Charlotte present well. Savory mousses are covered in Chapter 4 and the gelatin may be set with sweetened fruit purees as well. Fresh fruits or chocolate mousse may be presented inside an edible container. Piped and baked meringues or painted white chocolate "sacks" work well as edible containers, as seen in Color Plate 10. For the easiest edible cup, use Durkee or Pepperidge Farm puff pastry, or Athens Foods for mini or large filo dough shells. A rosette iron with several different molds can create baskets, butterflies, hearts, diamonds, and more. Simply heat the iron, dip it in a sweetened batter, and then plunge it into hot oil. The result, in just a minute or two, is a crisp, delicious, just-made pastry case of choice. Fill with sorbet, sherbert, vanilla ice cream, and seasonal fruits.

Brandy snaps may be rolled around a wooden spoon, metal cornucopia cone, or shaped into a tuille. The molding must be done quickly before the cookies have cooled, but they can always be returned to the oven for a minute to resoften if they become brittle. Decorations made of candied fruits, angelica, or mint, almond paste roses, or meringue mushrooms are eye appealing on any dessert. Arrangements on the tray or buffet should include a variety of desserts, in a myriad of forms with a range of light to decadent.

As far as props, do try to obtain a three-tiered tray for smaller cookies and pastries. Glass or plastic stands add height and thus greater perceived value. Individual servings of mousse are more elegant in wine or champagne glasses and more whimsical in espresso cups with a dollop of cream and a candy coffee bean (see Color Plate 10). A strawberry fan on the saucer would be a fine counterpoint of color and flavor.

Here, at last, is the famous Chocolate Decadent Killer Liability Mousse, which can be made in 7 minutes or less!

✳ CHOCOLATE DECADENT KILLER LIABILITY MOUSSE

YIELD: 8–10 servings

INGREDIENTS

8 ounces unsalted butter, softened   6 eggs

$1/4$–$1/3$ cup sugar or fructose

8 ounces semisweet or dark French
   Lanvin or Belgian chocolate

INSTRUCTIONS

Whip the butter and sugar in an electric mixer. Melt the chocolate in a microwave, 1 minute at a time, on the high setting. Remove bowl from microwave and gently shake to see if the chocolate has melted. Beat the chocolate into the butter mixture. Add the eggs *one at a time*, beating thoroughly after each. The mousse should become lighter and fluffier as each egg is added. Serve as described above.

Unusual plates, platters, and trays add a more aesthetic touch than regular round plastic disposables, but this of course depends upon the budget. Mirrors have long been used in culinary competitions but they are heavy and smear easily when guests take the dessert pieces.

Whatever the tray or buffet, weave in edible flowers for color and verve. Flowering herbs or even silk flowers as side props add color and artistry. Fabrics surrounding the serving dish furnish softness and texture as well as colors. Tossing streamers and confetti about the table or tray adds a festive touch. Keep a variety of tablecloths for seasonal and theme buffets. Even candle holders may prop up a dish of dessert!

Remember to garnish with a little sauce art for thunderbolts of color over the dessert or pooled lightly underneath. Try the tracing paper method to make silhouettes of a fork facing the product or doily stencils to make latticework over the entire cake. If you have no time to make your own desserts, it is acceptable to buy high-quality desserts from a local restaurant or bakery. Always mix rich desserts with a few lighter options and don't forget the garnish. PAPG prevails on any dessert tray or buffet—presentation, arrangement, propping, and garnishing.

DECADENT DESSERTS

These dessert concepts are a starting point of ideas to inspire you, from around the world. Samples recipes follow, with serving suggestions and variations.

Le Cordon Bleu Desserts

Brandied Fruit Flambé (see Color Plate 11)

Chocolate Ganache Tart w/Macadamia Crust

Cold Cordon Bleu Soufflé

Crème Anglaise

Crème Brûleé

Crepes Suzette

Floating Islands with Blackberry Coulis

Fresh Fruit Linzertorte

Fresh Fruit Sorbets, Gelatos, and Ices

Fruit Cream Parfait—layered fruit with Honeyed Ricotta Cheese

Fruited Melon Meringue

Hazelnut Meringue Hearts filled with Chocolate Decadent Mousse

Linzer Cream Wedges
Rose Pears in Chocolate Bath
Sweet Soufflé Omelet
White or Dark Chocolate 7-Minute Mousse in Espresso Cups

Southwest/Mexican Culinary Desserts
Border Ginger Cookies
Capirotada (Bread Pudding)
Coconut Flan with Amaretto
Drunken Bananas with Passionfruit Sauce
Flaming Bananas Foster
Fritters
Frozen Yogurt Sundae Buffet
Key Lime Mousse
Melon Trio with Mint and Cilantro
Mexican Rice Pudding
Mexican Strawberry Shortcake
Mexicali Turtle Sundae
Oversized Kahlua Chocolate Espresso Chip Cookie with Ice Cream and Fudge
Turtle Cream Puff with Ice Cream

Italian Desserts
Anise Biscuits (Biscotti al 'Ancice)
Baked Stuffed Peaches with Amaretti Cookies
Cannoli with various fillings
Crostata du Ricotta (Cheese Pie)
Fresh Figs with Champagne Sabayon
Fried Cookies (Cenci)
Genoa Cake with Strawberries and Zabaglione
Italian Bread Pudding (Budini di Pane)
Kadota Figs in Kirsch and Cream
Monte Bianco (Pureed Chestnuts and Cream)
Stovetop Cookies (Pizzelle)
Swans of Villa d'Este (Cream Puff Swans)

Pacific Rim Desserts
Any Fruit Mousse
Black Sticky Rice with Mango Puree
Chinese Almond Cookies
Chinese 5-Spice Cookies
Fortune Cookies
Ginger Frosted Fruit
Mango Apricot Fool or Whip
Sweet Dim Sum

Scandinavian Desserts
Baked Apples with Calvados
Bohemian Braid
Candied Fruit Stollen
Chocolate Walnut Date Torte with Berry and Banana Cream
Cinnamon and Apple Kuchen
Danish Rice Pudding with Sauce Melba
Lingonberry Crepes Flambe
Lucia Hot Cross Buns
Scandinavian Fruit Soup
Swedish Sugar Cookies
Swedish Tea Ring

Native American Desserts
Apple Brown Betty
Blue Corn Empanadas
Corn Fritters with Maple Syrup
Dessert Pizza with Berries and Linzer Crust
Fruit Cobbler Crunch
Indian Corn Cake and Pudding
Indian (Squaw) Bread
Mount St. Helen's Volcano
Rhubarb Cobbler
Sweet Potato Souffle

Chocolate Mousse Ideas

Shape hazelnut meringues into hearts and top with a sprinkling of candied red hearts.

Serve poached pears in thinned chocolate mousse.

Use chocolate mousse between layers of a cake or torte.

Create a layered mousse parfait with cobbler topping, amaretti, coconut, and chopped nuts with a dollop of whipped cream.

Serve a California Brownie with a reverse white chocolate brownie and nuts topped with frozen chocolate mousse and raspberry coulis.

Fill a cannoli with chocolate mousse.

Make a turtle creampuff with choux paste, frozen chocolate mousse, and sauces of chocolate and caramel with Spanish peanuts scattered over.

✱ ROSE PEARS IN CHOCOLATE BATH

The elegant appearance of this dessert on a plate or champagne glass belies its ease of preparation.

YIELD: 24 servings

INGREDIENTS

2 quarts plus 1 pint burgundy or white wine

$^1/_2$ cinnamon stick, broken

1 cup white sugar or brown sugar

6 whole cloves

1 tablespoon ginger

Rind of 2 oranges, grated

Rind of 2 lemons, grated

Rind of 2 limes, grated

$^1/_2$ cup orange juice (optional)

24 Bartlett pears, peeled and cored

15–20 ounces chocolate sauce

$^1/_2$ cup Cognac, Grand Marnier, or almond liqueur

GARNISH

Mint sprigs, kiwi slices, or candied violets

INSTRUCTIONS

In a medium saucepan, combine wine, sugar, cloves, ginger, orange rind, lemon rind, and lime rind. Bring to a boil. Add pears, reduce heat, and simmer just until fork tender, 8–10 minutes. Remove pears with a slotted spoon and cool.

Place whole or halved pear upright in each of 24 champagne or sherbet glasses. Mix chocolate sauce with Cognac or liqueur; drizzle over pears. Garnish with mint sprigs, kiwi slices, or candied violets.

✳ NUT-FILLED PEARS IN CHOCOLATE

Poach pears as directed. Halve pears horizontally, cutting in a sawtooth pattern to flute. Core and stuff each half with a mixture comprising equal amounts of chopped nuts, raisins, and dried dates or apricots. Reassemble pears and surround each one with chocolate sauce.

✳ ROSE PEARS WITH VANILLA CREAM

Poach pears as directed. Whip 1 pint whipping cream and fold into 1 pint vanilla pudding. Add 3–4 tablespoons Cognac. Place cream in bottom of serving glass. Top with pears and garnish with sprigs of mint.

✳ FRUIT CREAM PARFAIT

Vary the fruits and berries, fresh or frozen, and make the cream healthy or rich.

YIELD: 24 servings

INGREDIENTS

$3^1/_2$–4 pounds Neufchâtel or regular cream cheese, softened

2 pints whipping cream or canned evaporated skim milk, whipped

2 cups powdered sugar

4–5 tablespoons lemon or lime juice

Zest of 2 oranges, grated

Zest of 2 limes, grated

8–10 pounds fresh or frozen fruits, sliced

(Continued)

GARNISHES

Whipped cream or chopped nuts   Fresh mint sprigs
Candied violets

INSTRUCTIONS

With an electric mixer, beat cream cheese and whipping cream at high speed until light and fluffy. Reduce speed to low and add sugar, lemon or lime juice, orange rind, and lime rind.

Decorate an oversized plate with fruits, cream, and garnishes.

★ THREE-FRUIT COBBLER

Any fresh fruit in season or frozen fruit or berry may be substituted. Bake in half or full hotel pans or individual serving crocks.

YIELD: 8 servings

INGREDIENTS

2 cups all-purpose flour

2 cups quick-cooking oatmeal

4 ounces diced nuts

2 ounces butter, cut to chunks

$^1/_2$ teaspoon salt

1 teaspoon vanilla

$^1/_3$–$^1/_2$ cup honey

$^2/_3$ cup evaporated skim or evaporated regular milk

$^2/_3$ cup mixture of chopped nuts, raisins, and dried dates or apricots

2 pounds mixed fruits—apple, rhubarb, berry, or three-berry

$^1/_2$ teaspoon ginger

2 teaspoons lime juice

2 tablespoons cornstarch

INSTRUCTIONS

Preheat oven to 400°F. Combine flour, oatmeal, nuts, butter, and salt; mix until crumbly. Set aside. Combine remaining ingredients and place in pans or crocks. Top with cobbler mix and bake for 10–15 minutes. Serve warm or at room temperature.

✳ HAZELNUT MERINGUES

YIELD: 8 servings

INGREDIENTS

2 quarts water

Dash of cream of tartar

10 egg whites

1 cup hazelnuts or almonds, ground

Chocolate Mousse

Strawberry and mango purée sauces

Powdered chocolate

INSTRUCTIONS

In a large, wide frying pan, bring water and cream of tartar to a boil. Reduce heat to simmer.

Beat egg whites until they form soft peaks. Slowly beat in sugar until stiff peaks form. Fold in ground nuts.

Mound one eighth of the whites on a perforated skimmer and smooth gently into a domed island. Gently place skimmer on the surface of the hot water and hold until egg whites are released and float. Repeat for 7 more islands.

Do not let islands float into each other. Simmer them for 6–8 minutes or until egg whites are set. Drain on a clean towel; cool. Repeat with the next 7 islands.

To serve, chill 8 oversize plates. Spread chocolate mousse on chilled plates and center a hazelnut meringue on each. Mound with more chocolate mousse and garnish with lightning flashes or thunderbolts of fresh fruit purée sauces. Dust with a sprinkling of powdered chocolate.

DANISH RICE PUDDING

Vary this dessert by using different types of rice and assorted spices, fruits, and nuts. Mold and decorate it according to your imagination.

YIELD: 16 servings

INGREDIENTS

4 cups uncooked jasmine or basmati
   rice

2 teaspoons salt

$1^{1}/_{2}$ cups fructose or sugar

1 teaspoon cinnamon

1 teaspoon mace, nutmeg, or
   cardamom

1 quart plus 1 pint canned evaporated
   skim milk

1 pint skim milk (or as needed)

1 cup golden sultanas, currants, or
   raisins

1 cup almonds, hazelnuts, or walnuts,
   chopped

2 teaspoons vanilla

INSTRUCTIONS

Combine all ingredients in double boiler and cook, covered, stirring frequently until rice is tender and milk is almost absorbed, about 1 hour. Serve warm with Sauce Melba. Try molding pudding in decorative copper mold or terrine.

SAUCE MELBA

Whirl or process 12 ounces frozen raspberries or blackberries (for a variation) with $^{1}/_{4}$ cup powdered sugar or fructose. Strains seeds if desired, or thicken further with red currant jelly.

✳ GLASGOW SHORTBREAD

YIELD: 36 cookies

INGREDIENTS

$^1/_4$ cup sugar or fructose

2 cups flour, not sifted

$^1/_4$ cup rice flour

$^1/_2$ pound butter, unsalted, taken out
of refrigeration 15 minutes
before using

INSTRUCTIONS

Place sugar, flour, and rice flour on table. Lay on softened butter. Knead until mixture resembles a piece of putty. Pat or roll out to about $^3/_8$-inch thick. Prick dough with a fork. Cut with cookie cutter of choice.

Bake on an ungreased cookie sheet in 300°F. oven for about 20 minutes. Check for next 5–10 minutes until edges are golden brown. Place cookies on mesh rack to cool.

When cut cookies are cool, store in an air-tight container to preserve freshness and texture. Serve as a garnish on chocolate mousse or with fresh berries.

✳ VARIATION

Add lemon, lime, or orange zest to taste.

✴ ZABAGLIONE CREAM

Don't you hate it when you order Zabaglione and you know it came from a #10 can of vanilla pudding, complete with a chemical backwash in your mouth? Here is the classic cream. I did it from scratch when I was doing cross country trade shows for a National Brand manufacturer. This, of course, means booth cookery, off a hot plate, with no running water.

YIELD: 3 cups

INGREDIENTS

$^1/_2$ cup sugar

2 tablespoons flour

$^1/_4$ teaspoon salt

10 egg yolks

$^2/_3$ cup Marsala wine

2 teaspoons vanilla extract

2 cups heavy cream

6 egg whites

$^1/_2$ cup powdered sugar

INSTRUCTIONS

Combine sugar, flour, and salt in top of large double boiler on medium-high heat. Beat yolks, wine, and vanilla extract until the viscosity of a yellow ribbon and mix with sugar, flour, and salt, cooking until thick. Chill until cool but not set. Whip heavy cream until fully erect. Fold into yolks mixture. Beat whites until foamy and slowly add powdered sugar, beating all the while on high speed. Keep whipping until whites are tumescent. Add the whites to the cream mixture.

Layer with fresh berries, candied fruit, glaceed violets, poached peaches or pears, layered in strawberry shortcake or Genoa cake. Let your imagination fly to new heights.

⭐ LADYFINGERS

YIELD: 48 cookies

INGREDIENTS

6 eggs, separated

1 teaspoon vanilla

$^2/_3$ cup powdered sugar, sifted

1 cup cake flour, sifted

$^1/_4$ teaspoon salt

INSTRUCTIONS

Beat egg whites until fully engorged and erect, and gradually add in sugar.

In a separate bowl, whip yolks at high speed until a ribbony lemon color. Mix in vanilla and fold into egg whites. Fold in cake flour and salt.

Place heavy paper baking liners on heavy duty baking sheet. Fill pastry bag and plain hole tube with batter. Pipe 1 inch by $4^1/_2$ inch fingers. Sprinkle with powdered sugar. Bake at 350°F for 10–12 minutes. Remove with a long spatula to cool.

Place in elongated layers around periphery of glass bowl and fill with English trifle, serve on their own, or at a jaunty angle in Zabaglione Cream.

⭐ EGG-WHITE ALMOND CUSTARD

A lovely flan that is particularly smooth and inviting after a rich meal.

YIELD: 4 servings

INGREDIENTS

3 eggs

1 cup skim milk

1 cup evaporated skim milk

2 tablespoons maple syrup

2 tablespoons honey

3 tablespoons whole almonds, finely ground ($^1/_4$ cup total)

Pinch of salt

(Continued)

INSTRUCTIONS

Separate eggs and let whites come to room temperature. Refrigerate or freeze yolks for other uses.

Bring skim milk and evaporated skim milk to boiling point, add maple syrup, honey, and almonds and simmer gently for 1 minute. Remove from heat and cool to lukewarm.

Preheat oven to 325°F. Beat egg whites until frothy; add salt and continue to beat until stiff and fully engorged with air. Stir one third whites into milk mixture and fold in the remaining whites gently but thoroughly.

Pour flan into a shallow 9-inch pie dish or flan mold. Place in a wider pan filled with hot water. Bake 40–45 minutes, until knife inserted emerges clean. Cool to room temperature, then chill promptly for two hours before serving.

✳ HOT FRUIT COMPOTE

YIELD: 16 servings

INGREDIENTS

1 quart dry white wine, champagne or sparkling cider

2 ounces brown sugar (opt.)

1 teaspoon ginger

1 teaspoon nutmeg

1 teaspoon cinnamon

1 lemon, thinly sliced

1 lime, thinly sliced

4 small peaches or nectarines, sliced

4 small green apples, sliced

4 small red apples, sliced

2 fresh pears, sliced

INSTRUCTIONS

Combine all ingredients, except fruit, in a saucepan and bring to a boil. Reduce heat. Add fruit; cook and stir occasionally until tender, about 10 minutes. Serve warm.

CRANBERRY PUDDING WITH CITRUS HONEYED RICOTTA TOPPING

Tart berries explode in a sweet cakey batter, set off richly with a dressing of Whipped Citrus Honeyed Ricotta Topping, which is also great over fruits or layered with ladyfingers or biscotti.

YIELD: 4–6 servings

INGREDIENTS

CRANBERRY PUDDING

1 cup whole-wheat flour

1 cup all-purpose flour

1 tablespoon baking soda

$^1/_3$ cup honey

$^1/_4$ cup molasses

$^1/_2$ cup walnuts, chopped, toasted

$^3/_4$ cup hot water or evaporated skim milk

1 teaspoon lemon zest

1 teaspoon orange zest

1 cup fresh cranberries

CITRUS HONEYED RICOTTA TOPPING

1 pint nonfat sour cream or 1 pound cream cheese

1 pint nonfat ricotta cheese

Zest of 2 lemons

Zest of 2 oranges

Zest of 2 limes

Honey to taste

INSTRUCTIONS

Preheat oven to 350°F. Mix flour and baking soda. Stir in honey, molasses, and hot water all at once. When smooth, fold in walnuts, zests, and cranberries. Pour into a sprayed or buttered $1^1/_2$ quart baking dish. Bake for 25–30 minutes until brown on top and set. Serve at room temperature with topping.

Topping is made by whipping the sour cream or cream cheese, ricotta, citrus zests, and honey together. Store in refrigerator in a covered, dated container.

SOUR CREAM CRANBERRY PIE

This is a refreshing change from pumpkin and mince pies and a great finale to any fall or holiday meal. The tart cranberries explode in your mouth and are a great counterpoint of flavor and texture to the smooth, rich, custardy filling.

YIELD: 8 servings

INGREDIENTS

1 egg and 2 egg whites

$^{1}/_{2}$ cup honey

1 cup non-fat sour cream

2 tablespoons cranberry juice or
    lemon water

$^{1}/_{4}$ teaspoon salt

2 tablespoons flour

$1^{1}/_{2}$ pounds raw cranberries

9-inch pastry shell

$^{1}/_{4}$ cup flour (of choice)

$^{3}/_{4}$ cup oatmeal

1 cup brown sugar

1 cup chopped walnuts

Cinnamon, nutmeg, and allspice
    to taste

INSTRUCTIONS

Preheat oven to 425°F. With an electric mixer, beat the egg and whites in a small mixing bowl until thick. In a large mixing bowl, mix together the honey, sour cream, and juice. Gently stir in the eggs by hand.

Mix salt and flour with cranberries and delicately combine with egg mixture. Pour into pie shell. Combine flour, oatmeal, brown sugar, walnuts, and spices and sprinkle over top of the pie as a streusel topping.

Bake for 10 minutes at 425°F, then turn oven down to 375°F and continue baking for 25 minutes or until well browned. Cool completely on rack before cutting.

THE BEST PIE PASTRY DOUGH

YIELD: 8 or 9-inch single pie shell

INGREDIENTS

$1^1/_4$ cups all-purpose flour

$^1/_2$ teaspoon salt

1 tablespoon sugar

6 tablespoons chilled unsalted butter, cut into $^1/_4$-inch pieces

4 tablespoons chilled all vegetable shortening

3–4 tablespoons ice water

INSTRUCTIONS

Mix flour, salt, and sugar in food processor fitted with steel blade. Cut butter into small bits by cutting the stick of butter lengthwise with a large knife, rotating the stick ninety degrees and cutting again. Then cut the stick crosswise into one quarter inch pieces. Scatter butter over flour mixture, tossing to coat with some of the flour. Cut butter into flour with five 1-second pulses. Add shortening and continue pulsing until flour is pale and resembles coarse cornmeal with butter bits no larger than small peas, about four more 1 second-pulses. Turn mixture into chilled metal medium bowl.

Sprinkle 3 tablespoons ice water over mixture. With blade of rubber spatula, use folding motion to mix. Press down on dough with broad side of spatula until dough sticks together, adding up to 1 tablespoon more ice water if dough does not come together yet. Shape into ball with hands, then flatten into a 4-inch wide disc. Dust lightly with flour, wrap in plastic and refrigerate for 30 minutes before rolling. Dough should be rolled about one eighth inch thick.

✳ VARIATION

For a 10-inch regular or a 9-inch deep dish single pie shell, follow the same directions but increase flour by $^1/_4$ cup and butter by 2 tablespoons.

★ BAKED APPLES WITH CALVADOS

This is an easier but still delicious version.

YIELD: 24 servings

INGREDIENTS

24 baking apples

3 tablespoons butter

4 oranges

$^1/_3$ cup honey or maple syrup

$^1/_3$ cup dates, chopped

2 cups Calvados

20 whole cloves

20 star anise

4 sticks cinnamon, broken

1 cup shelled pistachios

INSTRUCTIONS

Preheat oven to 350–375°F. Core apples and peel top third of their skin. Place in baking dish. Divide butter, honey, and dates among apples. Zest oranges and set aside. Cut the zested oranges in half and squeeze juice over apples. Distribute chopped zest over all. Pour Calvados over and around apples in baking dish. Scatter spices overall. Coarsely chop pistachios and sprinkle over apples, making sure some go into the cavities.

Bake in oven for 30–45 minutes or until apples are tender when pierced with a fork. Baste every 15 minutes to keep apples from drying out if possible.

Remove from oven. Liquid in the dish should be reduced to a thickened, syrupy sauce. Place each apple on a dessert plate and spoon the sauce over and around apples. Serve warm or at room temperature, with or without ice cream.

MOCK CRÈME PÂTISSERIE

YIELD: 1 quart plus 1 pint

INGREDIENTS

1 pound nonfat cream cheese

1 pound nonfat quark

2 cups whipping cream or evaporated
   skim milk

Zest of 4 oranges

Zest of 4 lemons

Honey or fructose to taste

INSTRUCTIONS

Whip cheeses and set aside. Whip cream or chilled evaporated milk until soft peaks form. Fold whip into cheese mixture and flavor with citrus zest and sweetener of choice.

DEAL'S BEST DEAL LOW-FAT CHOCOLATE CARAMEL CAKE WITH LOW-FAT MOCHA CREAM FROSTING

Real Food Marketing Co. Inc. is a company in Kansas City, Missouri owned by renowned food inventor Bob Deal, with his partners Dan Carney and Patrick Vickers. Deal first founded Good Stuff Bakery in 1971 and supplied supermarkets, United Airlines, and Good Earth Restaurants, where we met. Back then all of his breads were natural and whole grain with a great flavor profile and texture. Bob's creations grace the menus of a number of restaurant chains today.

At Le Cordon Bleu, we learned how to make many rich cakes from scratch, but the techniques are rarely used these days. Here, however, is Bob's Low-Fat Chocolate Caramel Cake with Mocha Icing. Each slice has only 2.9 grams of fat.

YIELD: 16 slices

(Continued)

INGREDIENTS

LOW-FAT CHOCOLATE CARAMEL CAKE

3 tablespoons instant cornstarch

$^3/_4$ cup concentrated whey protein*

$5^1/_2$ cups cake flour

$1^3/_4$ cups nonfat cocoa

$^1/_2$ cup instant Jello chocolate pudding mix

5 teaspoons baking powder

2 tablespoons baking soda

$^1/_2$ teaspoon salt

$1^1/_8$ cups nonfat caramel

9 egg whites

$2^1/_2$ cups sugar

$2^1/_4$ cups water

$^1/_4$ cup nonfat dry milk

$^1/_4$ cup vanilla

LOW-FAT MOCHA CREAM FROSTING

1 cup sugar

2 cups water

$1^1/_2$ cups concentrated whey protein*

$^1/_2$ teaspoon vanilla

$^1/_8$ cup hot water

1 teaspoon instant coffee

4 whole eggs

4 tablespoons nonfat cocoa

2 tablespoons instant cornstarch

INSTRUCTIONS

LOW-FAT CHOCOLATE CARAMEL CAKE

Preheat oven to 375°F.

Sift and mix the cornstarch and concentrated whey protein with flour along with cocoa and pudding mix. Add baking powder, baking soda, and salt. Set aside.

Whip together the caramel, egg whites, sugar, and water. Slowly add the dry milk and vanilla. Add the dry mixture until well combined.

Divide batter among 3 9-inch pans. Bake for 27 minutes; test for doneness.

To cool the cakes quickly, freeze them for 30 minutes and frost.

LOW-FAT MOCHA CREAM FROSTING

Whip sugar, water, concentrated whey protein, and vanilla. Mix hot water with instant coffee and add to sugar mixture. Beat in eggs. Mix cornstarch and cocoa together and add slowly to frosting mixture.

*Freeze to cool down quickly (30 minutes) and then frost with palatte knife

SOUP AND SALAD BARS AND BUFFETS

4

Good soup and salad bars are popular with health-conscious diners because they provide a wide variety of healthy choices. The best operations constantly work to improve the quality of their products, the cleanliness of the operation, and customer service. Maintaining freshness is key, just as on steam table lines and with outgoing deli trays. Once deli trays are sent out, however, freshness becomes the responsibility of the client, whereas the work has just begun at salad bars and on soup and hot lines. Produce tends to wilt rather quickly. Quality-assurance techniques include shallow panning and water spraying.

Flawless presentation, arrangements, and the propping of food are central to the success of salad and soup buffets. Colorful salads stand on their own without major garnishing. Fresh products on trays or in crocks as well as surrounding the salad bar should be emphasized. Wooden crates, old-fashioned produce labels, and cascade arrangements of fruits and vegetables can be effective. Sprigs of fresh herbs, leaves, and edible flowers scattered across a white linen tablecloth conveys sprightly appeal at smaller buffets (see Color Plate 12).

Colorful food posters and table tents of monthly specials were placed throughout the stores of the Soup Exchange Restaurants and are still used at the Zoopa's and Fresh Choice chains. Mobile carts are often used for exhibition Caesar salad preparation, with personable cooks tossing salads to order. Unique serving containers and utensils are worth accumulating. While basic crocks may be all that your budget allows, enhance your buffet with one or two distinctive serving pieces. Instead of the ordinary black or beige plastic vessel, use an impressive urn or tureen. If even this is beyond your means, tie brightly colored napkins around the neck or top of the plain crocks. Clear Lexan or Cambro containers are often used for salad storage back of the line and for replenishing. These bins facilitate adherence to the first in, first out (FIFO) principle.

Oversized white and bright colored plates are best removed from a cooler by the guests themselves. Utensils may be wrapped in bright cloth napkins, tied with a contrasting bow, and placed upright in little clay flowerpots; breadsticks may be presented the same way.

A Fresh Choice restaurant procedure is the use of big plant sprayers; attendants run up and down the line spraying produce, salads, and garnishes with plain cold water. Tina Freedman, vice president for product development and purchasing at Fresh Choice, explains that keeping quality up to standard requires a constant training process.

Salad products and garnishes, such as blue cheese, that spill easily are set in front, making them easier to serve and clean up, according to Freedman. Items with the highest profit margin are served front and center and first on the line so that guests fill up on them right away.

If a salad or condiment container is too large, fill the base with a zippered plastic bag of ice or cold water and put the product on top. This touch provides a bountiful look with a minimum of waste, spoilage, and food cost. Shallow alley pans do the same thing for hot items.

Rick Gibony of Restaurants Unlimited, Inc. (RUI), original owner of Zoopa's in Seattle, speaks of the importance of the designed environment. Sophistication and quality are still apparent at Zoopa's. Crates, barrels with fresh produce, and silk or papier-mâché produce look alikes pop out in surprising places. Colorful signs and visual cues of fresh produce, bright lighting, multicolored tables, plates, and napkins, and just a fun bustle energize the operation (see Color Plate 13).

In southern California, Brandon Counts, assistant manager of Souplantation in Rancho Bernardo, shares a few industry solutions. "All our lettuce salads have a shelf life of twenty minutes and they are thrown out if not used up. We bring out whole heads of lettuce for produce propping. Other oversized platters are tilted toward the guests and replenished with fresh product from the back." Particular attention is paid to the heavy-traffic "scramble areas" where interactive pasta, soup, and bakery bars are hopping. Constant monitoring is evident, with crew members on top of spills and ready to answer salad bar questions. The best-quality products are purchased, the formulas followed, the servers friendly, and the entire restaurant is kept clean and shining.

You can accomplish this in your establishment by researching and reviewing new products and alternatives to your usual products. Sign on backup approved vendors to keep everyone consistent and honest. Approve by taste test, standardize, and document recipes and cross-train employees on each step. Besides costing the food and setting "pars," run a nutritional analysis on each formula for the benefit of guests and as a marketing strategy. New legislation requires a nutritional analysis for any dish with a heart-healthy icon or that is identified as low-calorie, low-cholesterol, or low-fat. Finally, hiring and training employees is an ongoing process. The process of internalizing concepts such as "customers are guests and always right" is continuous, as is the development of people skills.

THE SOUP SECTION

Hot soups on the buffet bar are among the most challenging to present and handle well. (Even Goldy, heroine of Diane Mott Davidson's culinary murder mysteries, claims good soup is labor intensive and volatile. "Cook it too long, and it gets like library paste. Cook it too little and it tastes like puddle water.")* Fortunately, many distinctive soups on the market now stand on their own or benefit by the addition of fresh chopped herbs, diced fresh vegetables, and garnishes.

Beware of overheating cream soups, as curdled cream has no eye appeal. Double-panned soups prepared au bain-marie always work. Viscosity of soups should be measured and monitored. If clam chowder is too thick and can't be thinned properly with milk or cream while still holding its flavor; it should be thrown out. The high-quality frozen or concentrated soups that are consistently good can be a big help. These can be transformed into signature or house soups with your additions: wine, sherry, liqueur, fresh herbs, vegetables, and condiment toppings.

A cycle of soups for seven days is the minimum needed for customer variety. Many delis and soup bars have three or four options each day. Soup, both in the making and in the garnishing, can be a terrific medium for using leftovers. Great soups hail from all regions of America. International soups are a traditional choice. Whatever the region or cuisine, all soups (and salads) benefit from your personal touch and presentation with other whole foods, flowers, and fabrics. Top with uniquely flavored or colored croutons for textural crunch. Swirl in compound butters or sprinkle soup with cheeses and seasonings. For bread, use rustic ryes, whole grains, or sourdough. Make use of fresh, seasonal and regional ingredients and highlight local farmers. Both fresh add-ins and garnishes lend color, flavor, and appeal.

---

* *The Grilling Season,* Bantam Dell Books © 1997.

With respect to propping and presentation, you can choose the new tureens from Bon Chef, which now carries ceramic-coated tureens in addition to stainless steel. They are a little more expensive but much more attractive. Whatever the tureen, prop the area with other charming containers for condiments, additional props, and whole foods that are ingredients of the dish. Have "Display Only" cards for the inedible props and whole food garnishes to make clear they are not for consumption.

Pay attention to and budget for props, condiments, and accompaniments. Surround the kettles with color by displaying fabrics, figurines, tinted bowls, sturdy whole foods from the soup, and even streamers along the cough guard. If the soup is Mexican style, drape a serape around the area, hang some castanets and post visual cues such as clay fish, bronze parrots, and papier-mâché pinatas. Play salsa music in the background and have the servers dress the part with colorful skirts or sombreros (see Color Plate 14).

You could sponsor a contest for children's drawings of their favorite soups, vegetables, or displays. Mat the art with colorful construction paper and display for the customers' enjoyment. Clip art is available right off your computer for added point-of-sale materials and interest. Posters and photographs are available from boards, councils, and commissions for various fruits, vegetables, and dairy products. A poster describing edible flowers is an educational conversation showpiece.

Tasty, appealing condiments can surround and adorn the container of soup for participatory garnishing by diners. Use small crock or authentic terra-cotta containers for soup embellishments. For a sopa de la casa, tortilla soup, or Mexican bean soup, provide sour cream or plain yogurt, plucked cilantro, sliced green onion, diced avocado dribbled with lime juice, grated cheeses of white and gold, and salsa fresca to add as toppings. Display as many colors, shapes, and textures as your time and budget permit.

Accompaniments of breads, breadsticks, croutons, and crackers offer customers a welcome number of choices. Great rustic breads with seed toppings and unusual grains are available from local bakers. Go for the quality your customers want. Bread is often a measuring stick for quality standards. Many restaurant reviewers and "foodies" scrutinize bread, which often creates the first impression of your restaurant's food. Showcase breads in baskets, vases, cleaned flowerpots, or more terra-cotta containers.

Whole food representing ingredients of the soup can be highlighted. The vegetables used to make Garden Patch Vegetarian Soup or minestrone are particularly vibrant. If an ice bed is available, design and display an arrangement of one whole fish and the other component of a seafood chowder, étouffée, or gumbo. Utilize the color chart from Chapter 1 for both whole produce displays, add-ins, garnishes, and condiment toppings.

Whet the customer's appetite with an attractive card describing the dish in tempting terms. Note whether the soup, salad, or dressing is vegetarian or low-fat; list some of the ingredients to add appeal and inform the curious customer. You can also give nutritional values and calorie counts. More conscientious diners than ever care about what they're eating.

Food history or an anecdote about where the dish came from is of interest to many customers. Table tents with provocative questions and humor give a conversational starting point for customers. For example, "Is the herb named coriander or cilantro? What countries use this herb? Name a recipe authentic to each cuisine," or "Have you ever eaten a chayote? It's called a *merliton* down in New Orleans. Do you know why? We have this delicious, healthy item featured raw on our salad bar and sautéed in our Creole Gumbo soup. Which way do you like it best?"

Each soup can also be garnished with bits of its ingredients. When Fresh Choice restaurants replenish their soups, they always stir in fresh raw diced vegetables from the original recipe. Management at Souplantation believes new soup added to depleted soup diminishes neither flavor nor eye allure.

Here are descriptions of wholesome soups that were developed for restaurant chains.

Spicy Tomato Rice Soup: A high-flavor-profile soup of the Southwest spiced with cumin, cloves, chili powder, and cinnamon. Delicious and hearty with brown or white rice, barley, spelt, or Kashi. A complete recipe is in this chapter.

Budapest Borscht: Actually a recipe from a trip to Soviet Georgia, this is a hearty vegetarian cabbage, potato, and beet soup. Use any classic borscht recipe but substitute vegetable broth for chicken or beef stock and purée most of the soup. Leave extra julienned cabbage and beets for texture and garnish.

Saffron Pumpkin Soup: A beautiful golden harvest soup made with fresh or canned pumpkin or with a variety of golden squashes and served in a baked or hollowed-out pumpkin. Orange zest and juice are less expensive than but as refreshing as saffron. See recipe on page 99.

Wild Rice, Cheese and Beer Soup: Fragrant with fresh vegetables and nutty brown and wild rice (lower food cost), this soup boasts the velvety richness of sharp cheddar cheese and a splash of dark microbrewed beer with the broth.

Lemony Lebanon Lentil Soup: Add Swiss chard, potatoes, cumin, cilantro, and lemon to your favorite lentil soup; omit the traditional spices.

Vegetarian Garden Patch Minestrone: This colorful, healthy soup features fresh al dente vegetables and a judicious use of fresh herbs typical of Italy.

Creamy Herbal Walnut Soup: This distinctively slate-colored soup is very aromatic. The "cream" is evaporated skim milk, part of the roux is nonfat dry milk, and the herbs are thyme, parsley, and basil.

Potato Leek Soup: A vichyssoise becomes Potage Bonne Femme (good woman's soup) when served heated.

Ratatouille Soup: Thin this vegetable cassoulet with vegetable or chicken broth.

Corn and Cheddar Chowder: This thick soup also includes potatoes and optional beer. Roasting or grilling the corn increases its caramel flavor, chewy texture, and brix level.

Soybean Soup Bistro-Style: This is a quick soup to make if the soybeans are cooked ahead or bought canned. Pack it with nutritious and delicious vegetables.

Mushroom Barley Soup: A creamy, rich brown soup with a variety of domestic and wild mushrooms, red onions, carrots, and celery. It has a musky flavor and the nutty taste of barley.

Seafood Bisque: A classic soup with a low-calorie, low-cholesterol, and low-cost twist: evaporated skim milk is used for heavy cream and the result tastes just as good.

Cream of Anything Soup: The quick and easy base is tested and refined and low in calories, cholesterol, and cost. Any vegetables past their prime may be blended with garnish and flavoring variations: broccoli, carrot, watercress, spinach, chard, and Carolina greens, even plain lettuces for a delicate spring green. Many cream soups are excellent cold as well.

Cold soups are fun to style and prop. Bright fruit purées are spectacular in a whole watermelon. Clear containers or vivid Fiestaware can add a rainbow of colors. Try a classic Swedish Blueberry soup with lemon wheels and sprigs of mint in clear cut glass. From the renowned apple-growing region of France comes a Cream of Normandy soup featuring tart red apples, a jot of curry, and a splash of lemon juice—or Calvados (Normandy apple brandy), if your budget allows. Serving this soup in oversized apple tureens or individual hollowed apples would be very attractive.

Creamy cantaloupe and honeydew soups can be presented side by side in a tureen or serving dish. Pour the soups simultaneously into each half of the bowl, or use a foil-wrapped cardboard in the center and pull it out later. Potage Bonne Femme and Creamy Roasted Red Pepper Soup (p. 104) makes another handsome pair. Swirling in a bit of sour cream adds a pleasing marbled effect and berry purée is marvelous for the melon soups.

Try serving papaya-cantaloupe soup in fluted cantaloupe shells, any melon soup in a mini-apple tureen, or cucumber mint soup in an acorn squash. These thicker fruit soups often support the weight of thinly sliced citrus wheels, golden raspberries, small strawberry fans, or blueberries. For a lighter effect, drop in edible flowers such as pansies, herb blossoms, miniature carnations, or nasturtiums. For real ease, a quick sprinkling of flower petals, paprika, parsley, or lemon zest makes a charming garnish.

Utilize the bed of ice chilling the fruit soups to provide a natural scene of whole and cut fruits and garnishes. Set soup ingredients such as slivers of melon, wedges of pineapple, and English cucumbers in the ice. Imagine the cucumbers as fresh growing asparagus protruding from the soil, ready to be snapped off at the base. Whole berries, sliced strawberries, and citrus wheels on ice allow guests to garnish at will.

★ SPICY TOMATO RICE SOUP

First developed for Sunset *magazine in 1975 and used by the Avocado Board, and Souplantation, this soup can be easily varied and garnished.*

YIELD: 24 1-cup servings

INGREDIENTS

1 ounce butter (or use spray oil)

3 medium red onions, minced

104-ounces canned tomatoes, all-purpose, crunched

$2^1/_2$ quarts vegetarian broth

2 quarts cooked brown or white rice or barley (or mixture thereof)

2 tablespoons paprika

1 tablespoon sugar

1 tablespoon basil

3–4 bay leaves

$^1/_2$–1 teaspoon chili powder

$1^1/_2$ teaspoons cloves, ground

$1^1/_2$ teaspoons nutmeg, grated

1 cup parsley, minced

(Continued)

GARNISHES FOR INDIVIDUAL SERVINGS

1 heaping tablespoon avocado, diced   Sour half-and-half or plain yogurt
1 lemon slice

INSTRUCTIONS

In a large stockpot, melt butter or spray oil over medium heat. Add red onions and sweat, covered, until limp, about 5 minutes. Add tomatoes, broth, rice or barley, paprika, sugar, basil, bay leaves, chili powder, cloves, nutmeg, and parsley. Simmer, covered for 15 minutes. Remove from heat and discard bay leaves.

Add garnishes to bowls if serving individually or display them near soup pot for guests to serve themselves. Sliced green onion, plucked cilantro, grated cheese, and salsa roja or verde are also authentic garnishes for this hearty, low-cost soup.

★ SOPA DE LA CASA

YIELD: 20 1-cup servings

INGREDIENTS

1 ounce butter

Oil spray on nonstick pot

2 medium red or yellow onions, diced

4–5 cloves (as desired) garlic, minced

10 medium carrots, peeled and diced

5 zucchini, cubed

5 crookneck squash, cubed

5 pounds cooked refried black beans

2 quarts chicken or vegetable broth

4 whole cooked chicken breasts, cut to thin strips (optional)

2–3 teaspoons chili powder (optional)

1 teaspoon dried oregano leaves or 1 tablespoon fresh chopped oregano

1 teaspoon red pepper flakes

1 teaspoon cumin

Salt to taste

Black pepper, freshly ground to taste

GARNISHES

Cilantro sprigs

Salsa fresca

Cheddar cheese, grated

Jalapeño jack cheese, grated

Radishes, sliced

Avocado, diced

Sour cream or quark

Chives, freeze-dried

Olives, sliced

Lime wedges

INSTRUCTIONS

Oil spray a large nonstick pot or Dutch oven; heat over medium heat. Add onion, garlic, carrots, zucchini, and crookneck squash; sauté until all but carrots are tender, 4–5 minutes. Add beans, broth, chicken, and seasonings and simmer, covered, 10–15 minutes.

Garnish as desired or serve with a choice of toppings.

★ SAFFRON PUMPKIN SOUP

Butternut or acorn squash may be substituted for pumpkin and 2 tablespoons dark rum for the saffron. Float a dab of vanilla yogurt and minced orange zest or diced peaches. This can be very quick with canned pumpkin too.

YIELD: 24 1-cup servings

INGREDIENTS

1 bunch green onion, thinly sliced

1 large red onion or sweet white onion, diced

1 quart plus 1 pint vegetable broth

4 quarts pumpkin, seeded and coarsely chopped

3–4 bay leaves

Generous pinch of saffron

1 teaspoon freshly ground white pepper

1 pint evaporated or regular skim milk, scalded

(Continued)

GARNISHES

Lime or lemon slices

Quark, nonfat sour cream, or
   vanilla yogurt

Orange zest, minced, or peaches,
diced

INSTRUCTIONS

In a large stockpot, cook the green and red or white onions in the vegetable broth until tender. Stir in the pumpkin, bay leaves, saffron, and white pepper. Cover and simmer for 30 minutes. Discard bay leaves.

In a blender or robot coupe, blend soup in batches until smooth. Stir in skim milk. Serve immediately with paper-thin slices of lime or lemon and a dollop of quark, nonfat sour cream, or yogurt.

✱ VARIATION

Eliminate green onion and add 8 tart green apples, cored and chopped, 2–4 cups apple juice, cinnamon, and freshly grated nutmeg to taste.

✱ CREAM OF ANYTHING SOUP

YIELD: 20 1-cup servings

INGREDIENTS

1 ounce butter

1 ounce canola oil

2 large red or yellow onions,
   roughly chopped

2 ounces flour

1 cup nonfat dry milk

3–4 cans evaporated skim milk,
   13 ounces each

1 quart skim milk or vegetable broth

4 pounds vegetables; carrots or celery,
   finely chopped; broccoli or
   cauliflower, broken into flowerets;
   mushrooms, coarsely chopped;
   5–6 bunches spinach or watercress;
   4 bunches chard, kale, sorrel,
   dandelion, or combination
   of greens; fresh baby asparagus

GARNISHES

Amontillado dry sherry

Nutmeg, freshly grated

Thyme leaves

Lemon wheels

Sour cream or quark

INSTRUCTIONS

In a large nonstick stockpot, sauté onion in butter and oil until softened. Stir in flour and dry milk and cook until bubbly. Gradually add 2 cans evaporated milk and 2 cups skim milk or broth, stirring well to combine. Add vegetables and bring to boiling point. Reduce heat and simmer until vegetables are tender, about 10 minutes (root vegetables are longer cooking). Season to taste with fresh herbs as suggested below.

Cool soup (This is important—hot soup will blow lid off blender), then purée in blender in batches until smooth. Stir in remaining liquids to desired viscosity. Serve hot or chilled; garnish imaginatively.

SUGGESTED SEASONINGS AND GARNISHES

Carrot Soup: Stir into each serving $^1/_2$–1 teaspoon fresh thyme leaves or minced dill. Serve in condiment containers near soup tureen.

Cauliflower Soup: Swirl in shredded sharp golden cheddar cheese.

Mushroom Soup: Vary the species of mushrooms used. Stir in plain yogurt or quark. Grate fresh nutmeg over soup.

Broccoli Soup: Stir in dry sherry to taste. Add lemon wheels and dollops of sour cream.

Watercress or Sorrel Soup: Garnish each serving with lime wheels, quark, or yogurt, and a sprinkling of nutmeg or paprika.

Spinach Soup: Stir into each serving $^1/_2$ teaspoon thyme leaves. Garnish tureen with sieved hard-cooked egg yolk.

Country Greens Soup: I developed a North Carolinian cuisine (when I lived there one year) that used local ingredients, including dandelion greens, collards, and Swiss chard. These can be pureed for a Spring Green Soup, served hot or cold.

Asparagus Soup: Stir in a little fino dry sherry and garnish with lemon wheels, a dollop of quark, and a jaunty asparagus tip.

POTAGE SAINT-GERMAIN

This light soup is ideal as an hors d'oeuvre sipping soup or first course. The delicate spring-green color is an aesthetic element that pleases the eye first—then the green pea and sherry flavors please the palate! This is a classic, served hot or cold. I learned this favorite at the Cordon Bleu in 1973. It is much healthier than most of their soups.

YIELD: 20 1-cup servings

INGREDIENTS

1 tablespoon butter or spray oil as needed

4 large carrots, peeled and diced

1–2 bunches scallions, sliced

2 ounces flour

4–5 cans evaporated skim milk, 13 ounces each

1$^1/_2$–2 cups vegetable or chicken broth

5 pounds frozen peas, thawed

$^1/_2$ cup sherry, fino dry or dry white wine

GARNISHES

Parsley, minced
Lemon slices or striped wheels

Nonfat sour cream or yogurt
Chives, freeze-dried

INSTRUCTIONS

In a large nonstick stockpot, melt butter or spray oil and sauté carrots and scallions. Add flour and cook, stirring, until bubbly. Add the milk and broth and bring to a boil, stirring occasionally. Add peas, reduce heat, and simmer until carrots are tender, about 6 minutes. Whirl the soup in a robot coupe or blender, one portion at a time, until smooth. Return purée to pan, stir in sherry to taste, and heat through.

Garnish with minced parsley, lemon slice wheels, and a dollop of sour cream or yogurt with a sprinkling of chives.

✳ SOULMATE CHICKEN SOUP

There are many wonderful variations of this nurturing soup, all of them popular.

YIELD: 80 1-cup servings

INGREDIENTS

1 gallon plus $^1/_2$ gallon water

$^1/_4$ –$^1/_2$ pound dried porcini mushrooms (optional)

1 ounce butter or margarine

$2^1/_2$ pounds carrots, peeled, sliced diagonally

2 pounds celery, washed, sliced diagonally

$1^1/_4$ pounds yellow or red onions, peeled, diced

1 pound parsnips, peeled, diced

1 pound soup greens, cleaned, cut to chiffonade

$^1/_2$ gallon white wine

3.5 ounces chicken base

$5^1/_2$ pounds chicken meat, cut $1^1/_2 \times {}^1/_2 \times {}^1/_2$ inches

3 ounces parsley, chopped

1 tablespoon kosher salt

2–3 tablespoons dillweed, freshly minced (or 1 tablespoon dried)

2 teaspoons coarse ground pepper

2 teaspoons liquid hot pepper

$2^1/_2$ pounds wide egg noodles

Quark or nonfat sour cream (optional), as needed

INSTRUCTIONS

Simmer dried mushrooms in $^1/_2$ gallon of water for 15 minutes. Scoop out, pat dry, and slice thinly. Set aside.

Sauté carrots, celery, onions, parsnips, and soup greens in butter for 5 minutes in steam-jacketed kettle or large stockpot. Add reserved mushrooms, remaining water, white wine, chicken base, chicken meat, parsley, salt, dillweed, ground pepper, and liquid hot pepper and simmer 20 minutes. Add noodles and simmer 8–10 minutes or per package directions.

Stir in sour cream or quark as a liaison before serving.

✳ CREAMY POTATO-PEPPER SOUP

The pears add a subtle sweet fruitiness to this peppery soup. Garnish at will with sour cream, chopped fresh parsley, and a lemon wheel with a julienne twist of roasted red pepper.

YIELD: 12 cups

INGREDIENTS

1–2 tablespoons unsalted butter

2 large onions, chopped

4 cloves garlic, minced

2 Russet Idaho potatoes, peeled
   and diced

28 ounces roasted red peppers,
   drained, patted dry, and chopped

5 cups chicken broth

2 16 ounce cans pear halves, packed
   in juice, drained and chopped

Sea salt and freshly ground pepper
   to taste

INSTRUCTIONS

Melt butter in stock pot, and sweat onions and garlic until softened. Add potatoes and peppers and saute 10–15 more minutes. Stir in broth and pears. Reheat. Puree until nearly smooth with some chunks, by pulsing.

✳ COLD CHERRY SOUP (KIRSCHEN KALTSCHALE)

A small amount of fresh orange juice may fully bring out the flavor. Check and re-season for the tartness of the cherries.

YIELD: 6 1-cup servings

INGREDIENTS

1 pint sour cherries with juice	1 or 2 whole cloves
1 pint water	1 small piece of stick cinnamon
1 cup Merlot	1 teaspoon cornstarch
2 tablespoons lemon juice	6 mint sprigs
$1/4$ cup sugar or honey	6 lemon slices

INSTRUCTIONS

Reserve 6 cherries for garnish. Reserve 2 tablespoons water. Place remaining cherries, water, Merlot, lemon juice, honey or sugar, cloves, and cinnamon stick in a large enough pot; bring to a boil. Reduce heat and simmer briefly.

Mix cornstarch with reserved water. Add to simmering soup, stirring well. The soup should be of a thin consistency but cornstarch will aid in achieving a fine patina and sheen. Strain to remove spices. Adjust seasonings. Chill well.

Serve in chilled cups with cherry, mint sprig, and lemon slice.

★ PAPAYA-CANTALOUPE SOUP

This soup was often made aboard a 60-foot Gulf Star in Newport, Rhode Island, and later on motor yachts, cruising the Cays of the Caribbean. It's both bright and cooling for a hot day anywhere—land or sea, for luncheon or breakfast.

YIELD: 16 1-cup servings

INGREDIENTS

4 papayas	1 quart evaporated skim milk
8 medium cantaloupes	1 teaspoon cinnamon
1 pint nonfat quark or plain yogurt	1 teaspoon nutmeg, grated
1 pound nonfat cream cheese	

(Continued)

GARNISHES

Mint sprigs   Quark
Lemon or orange wheels

INSTRUCTIONS

Peel and seed the papayas. Flute the cantaloupes in half and remove seeds. Scoop out almost all of the flesh. Blend quark or yogurt, cream cheese, evaporated milk, cinnamon, nutmeg, and flesh of cantaloupes in blender or robot coupe in batches until smooth and creamy, then chill.

Fill fluted melon halves with soup and garnish with mint, citrus wheels, and quark.

✶ COOL CUCUMBER MINT SOUP

Cool soups are often overlooked, but they make a refreshing change of pace in summer months. You can easily turn this soup into a mousse or mold and serve with salmon, shrimp, or crab.

YIELD: 16 servings

INGREDIENTS

2 pints plain yogurt

1–2 pounds cream cheese

8 cucumbers, peeled and coarsely chopped

1 tablespoon plus 1 teaspoon lemon juice

$^1/_4$ cup mint, freshly chopped

1 pint cold club soda

Salt and freshly ground white pepper to taste

> **INSTRUCTIONS**
>
> Place yogurt and cream cheese in food processor. Briefly whirl to blend; remove half of this mix. Place cucumber, lemon juice, mint, and club soda in batches in processor and process off and on until all the cucumber is finely diced. Season to taste with salt and pepper.
>
> Serve from kettle, tureen, or edible containers.

SALAD BARS AND BUFFETS

This subject is close to my heart, as I developed a number of food formulas for major West Coast salad bar chains in my career. What an adventure it was for health-conscious diners to see the abundance of traditional and exotic fruits, vegetables, greens, grains, and beans in international and regional salads—and all arranged beautifully.

Salads are important to healthy eaters of all kinds. Weight lifters, dieters, individual and team athletes, and professionals on the run love the variety of displays and ease of eating in well-planned and well-presented salad bars. Chefs get real pleasure from seeing guests light up at the sight of the opulent display—and then the taste of their fantastic food. I enjoyed using the then-unusual jicama, blood orange, kumquat, quinoa, spelt, triticale, millet, wheat berries, buckwheat, and couscous as ingredients and garnishes. Exploiting their color and visual appeal when they were in season or on special made this approach cost-effective.

Salad bars are basically healthy, if high-fat dressings are not abundantly ladled over the greens. Heart-healthy prepared salads with quality controls implemented in each standardized recipe provide diners with even more healthy options.

At the restaurants where I worked, dressings were presented in a variety of cruets, crocks, and bottles with descriptions of low-fat alternatives. I developed a line of flavored and herb-infused vinegars that looked good on the shelf behind the salad bar and could also be used for dressing. This is an example of an edible prop. Dressing names and nutritional values were listed neatly.

However, the operators put more and more profit centers in: scoop and bake muffins, soup bars, frozen yogurt and dessert bars, and too many exhibition kitchens. A panacea restaurant can overwhelm the original concept.

One chain, however, did have a great system for quality control. The FATT system involved regularly checking the *f*lavor, *a*ppearance, *t*emperature, and *t*exture of the product. The FATT technique was used by Zoopa's. Other salad bar chains that valued quality used FIFO systems and dating, whether color coded or simply labeled.

You should check salads often for flaccidity and overmarination. Periodically check and replenish garnishes too. Taste all tested recipes before serving. Implementing these standards leads to outstanding quality.

Marinades and dressings should be kept to low levels in each bowl of salad. Watery, oozing dressing does not make a palate-pleasing salad. In fact, it's a red flag for salads that have sat too long. Frequent checking of all products for quality of flavor, appearance, temperature, and texture, especially before peak service (or sending out) must be stringently implemented. Personally walk the line to make sure all is up to standard.

A buffet table will suffice for a salad bar if space is limited or guests few. Hidden Creek Dude Ranch in Harrison, Idaho, served up a cozy little salad bar right next to their massive stone fireplace for enhanced ambience. All the vegetables and greens, coupled with homemade breads and a variety of both rich and low-fat dressings, made for a nutritious lunch (see Color Plate 15).

Outdoor salad buffets can be highly successful too. Along the Salmon River in Idaho, a colorful display was set up right on a sandbar. Rivers Odessey West showed just how creative camping cuisine can be. These techniques can be adapted for any off-premise catering event.

All mixed salads were prepared a day early and stored in plastic containers in coolers for the flavors to meld overnight. When it came time to serve the meal, colorful lightweight crocks were displayed on a festive tablecloth. The river guides lent their personal touch to the garnishes by arranging whole kalamata olives on a bed of alfalfa sprouts and folding back lengthwise-sliced kosher pickles around the perimeter. The effect was a blooming edible flower.

Whatever the level of service, salads offer the most opportunities for arrangements in edible containers and decorations. At one of my first jobs, remembering Le Cordon Bleu's dictum "Keep it simple," I highlighted each salad with a food item from the salad itself in a startling way—a large vegetable flower, cut-outs of the then unknown jicama, chayote slices, a skewered slice of cheese shaped in a heart, a dusting of edible flower petals. Often the mixed salads showed well on their own, offering color and decorative appeal in the cut and shapes of the vegetables. In other cases, a rolled thin rye crisp was presented upright with a bouquet of edible greens and flowering herbs spraying out like a flower arrangement.

This experience of using exotic vegetables, new shapes and garnishes, and edible containers serve me well later. For various books, manufacturers, restaurant chains, and salad bars it was easy and exciting to develop composed salads and dressings with variations on the original salad themes.

Always keep your notes, designs, recipes, and photos from every job. These concepts may be revived, at any time, with a new twist, arrangement, or garnish.

There are no real new recipes—just three major changes and you have a new formula. A short list of more ideas could include:

Bell pepper rings of any and all colors

Long and fine julienne of any root vegetables

A confetti scattering of chopped flower petals

Thin ribbon slices of English cucumber, carrot, and daikon

Red onion rings with a mound of sprouts in the center

Paper-thin slices of root vegetables soaked in ice water

Leaves of banana, avocado, lemon, or fig

A wreath of mixed squashes surrounding the display urns

Chopped or whole raw or roasted nuts for crunch

A colorful display indicates the freshness and artistry of your salad bar. If a theme, region, or country is used as the concept, utilize typical props, music, and even server costumes. Introduce fruits and vegetables typical of the region.

Try some of the distinctive and easy garnishes shown in Chapter 2. Just a bouquet of turnip calla lilies laid gently across the ice bed will cause guests to smile at your creative touch.

SIGNATURE SALADS

International Salads

These concepts were originally developed for a Northwest chain to implement as a product line extension. Each formula met corporate criteria with respect to the equipment package, required employee skill level, cold table holding capability, time to complete (35–45 minutes), food cost ($20–$30 per 4–9 quarts), and, of course, flavor, appearance, texture, and temperature. A chef demo station/cold pasta bar gives guests the choice of pasta, filling mix, and sauce (see Color Plate 16.) The chef can explain each option and how it's made.

Gado Gado: This is a colorful Indonesian vegetarian vegetable salad, a classic with spicy peanut sauce, coconut milk, and lemon zest dressing.

Pacific Rim Pasta Salad: Fusion cuisine yields this eclectic mix of flavors, colors, and textures that can be served with fish, chicken, or beef.

Serbian Salad: Cucumbers and peppers are favorites in the former Yugoslavia. This dish may be made richer and more substantial with the addition of tofu, sour cream, or shrimp.

Chinese Noodle Salad with Roasted Eggplant: This salad is superb, simple to prepare, and its ingredients keep well for several days in the refrigerator. It features flavors of sesame, balsamic vinegar, cilantro, ginger, garlic—and it's vegetarian.

Syrian Salad: Romaine is combined with cucumber, radishes, peppers, tomatoes, red onion, feta cheese, potatoes, chicory or escarole, and an intensely flavored, delicious dressing.

Pasta Sea Vegetable Salad with Lemon Tahini Sauce: This unusual dish is low-fat and vegetarian and uses buckwheat noodles, tempeh, vegetables, hijiki seaweed, and interesting additions such as seitan, lemongrass, and blue-green algae.

Rodbetsallad: This dish is from Sweden—not surprisingly, it has beets, cabbage, and an interesting Russian dressing of homemade chili sauce, mayonnaise, and cream.

Celery Root Salad: Celery root is tasty and stands up well on the buffet table. You can sneak in parsnips, turnips, and other economical root vegetables as well. The dressing is a lemon Dijon cream base. Sliced green onion or julienned fennel, chard, or spinach adds a bright dash of green.

Conventional Salads

California Crunch Health Slaw: Use both red and green cabbage with wheat germ. Get additional crunch from sunflower or pumpkin and celery seeds and the succulent sweetness of red and green grapes. Add a mango lime dressing.

Spicy Dijon Coleslaw: Traditional cabbage and slaw ingredients stand up to the intense dressing. Optional: bay shrimp.

Solana Beach Seafood Seashell Salad: This salad can embrace any shape pasta, any vegetable, perhaps cut-out stamps of multicolored bell peppers and squashes, your seafood of choice, and a lemony low-fat vinaigrette. Chicken broth is substituted for some of the olive oil and lemon juice and zest for some of the balsamic vinegar. Fresh, colorful, light, and easy—this makes a great salad.

Sweet-and-Sour Four-Bean Salad: Mix this effortless sauce from Chapter 3 into canned bean salad. Vary the beans with cranberry, flageolets, adzuki beans, and hominy.

Garden-Fresh Vegetables and Rices: Try plain white rice, brown basmati rice, Kashi, and bulgur with a profusion of vegetables and fresh dilled creamy dressing based on nonfat quark, ricotta, cream cheese, or yogurt.

Bow-Ties or Fusilli with Tuna, Broccoli, and Roasted Spicy Red Peppers: The name says all the ingredients, but the sparkling roasted red pepper dressing comes from the spread and dip variation included in Chapter 3. Simply thin with red wine or fruit vinegar and extra-virgin olive oil. This dish has the spicy but compatible components that yield a rich, bold flavor profile.

Mainstay Macaroni Salad: This is an interesting combination of whole-wheat elbow noodles and curly egg pasta, dilled mayonnaise dressing, and julienned steamed vegetables.

Potato Salads

There are many regional and international variations of this traditional favorite.

Russian Potato Salad: New potatoes, dill, eggs, beets, and capers gently blended with horseradish, sour cream, or quark, and Dijon or Pommery mustard.

Mexican Potato Salad: Chili strips, tostada seasoning, sour cream, salsa, and cilantro. Add color and crunch by scattering crushed red, blue, and yellow tortilla chips over the top.

German Potato Salad: Hearty baked potato salad with bacon, onions, vinegar, celery seed, and hard-cooked eggs. This is a non-mayonnaise dressing.

Susan's Spa Cuisine Potato Salad: Yellow Finn or Yukon Gold new potato salad with chives, fresh fennel, watercress, and a dressing of light mayonnaise with buttermilk or plain yogurt.

Protein Showtime Salads

Showtime salads can be demonstrated in front of guests, whether they involve putting the dressing together from mise en place ingredients, arranging a composed salad, or carving and placing a few distinctive garnishes. Each formula requires only 35–45 minutes to prepare 6–9 quarts and costs $40.00 to $45.00. Your guests can see how fresh these salads are when made right in front of them.

Seafood Louis with Low-Fat Louis: This is a classic composed salad with a pinwheel of bright flavors: hard-cooked eggs, tomato wedges, California avocado, shrimp, surimi crab, and the best and easiest low-calorie Louis dressing ever.

Jambalaya Chilled Salad: This utilizes millet and rices and the basic Creole ingredients of fish, chicken, and sausage. It is less expensive than a chilled paella.

Shrimp, Chicken, or Beef Fajita Salad: Generate a classic fajita mix with any protein, garlic, onions, and sweet peppers splashed with lime juice. Traditionally served with warm flour tortillas, guacamole, salsa, and refried beans, this can also be served hot and snapping over a crisp green salad. A good choice for a sizzling showtime salad.

Seafood and Artichoke Salad: Combine an extraordinary fresh lemon vinaigrette with assorted seafood, artichoke hearts, and kalamata olives.

Mexican Shrimp Salad: Fat little shrimp and chubby chunks of Haas avocado meet a zesty dressing of cilantro and lime with surprisingly complex results. With the additions of red onion, oranges, and cucumbers for color and crunch, the last touch could be a topping of crushed blue corn tortilla chips.

Asian Chicken Salad: This salad features a colorful variety of fresh steamed oriental vegetables with an authentic dressing of tamari, ginger, rice wine vinegar, and dark sesame oil.

Cajun Chicken Salad: Seasonal but bright red and bursting with the spicy flavors of traditional Cajun cookery, this salad balances the fires of peppers with the refreshing coolness of tropical papaya (or mango, or avocado).

Smoked Turkey Salad: This versatile salad works well with chicken, duck, or turkey. It is a complex, savory salad, a study in contrasts of taste and texture—chewy, with snippets of sherried sundried tomatoes, smoky fingers of turkey, crunchy nuts, and crisp, tart Granny Smith apples.

Curried Chicken Waldorf Salad: This is a lightly curried Waldorf mix; add chicken or turkey for more protein and profit.

Creamy Fruity Spelt Tabouli: This is a tasty twist on a classic Waldorf and tabouli. Any apple and dried fruit can work with zested orange and tangerine, toasted almonds, parsley, and mint.

CALIFORNIA TRENDY CHIC SALAD

YIELD: 24 servings

INGREDIENTS

4 pounds artichokes, frozen

18 roma tomatoes, cut in 6 wedges

8 ounces kalamata olives, drained
   and sliced

3 tablespoons zest of lemon rind

2 cups lemon juice

$^1/_2$ cup walnut or olive oil

12 ounces goat cheese, sliced into
   $^1/_2$-inch thick slices

Parsley, minced

6 heads of romaine, cut to chiffonade

12 ounces walnuts, chopped and
   toasted

INSTRUCTIONS

Thaw artichokes. Combine with tomatoes, olives, and zest. Stir in juice and oil.
Chill for 2 or more hours.

   Dust goat cheese with minced parsley; broil for 1 minute.

   Arrange artichoke mixture on chiffonade of romaine. Drizzle mango lime
dressing over salad (see recipe in dressings section below) and serve additional
dressing separately. Garnish with broiled goat cheese (broiled briefly under a salamander until golden) and top with toasted walnuts.

MOUSSES AND MOLDS

Just like props, unique molds for mousses and gelatin salads can be found at
garage sales, auctions, antique and junk shops, and thrift stores. Some companies
that create garnishing stamps can design a mold featuring your logo, theme, or
mascot. Even a ring mold, properly flavored and garnished, can invoke the oohs
and ahs of your customers.

   One of the best uses for spray release oils is for thoroughly and evenly coating the inside of molds. This technique makes it much easier to get into every crevice, than brushing, toweling, or fingering does. New planet-friendly pump sprays can be filled with your oil of choice. The pump is powerful and provides complete coverage with ease.

Prepare mousse of your choice; pour it into a well-oiled mold. To set it thoroughly, place mousse in refrigerator overnight, which also allows flavors to amalgamate. When unmolding before service, quickly plunge bottom of mold into a bath of warm water. Run a butter knife between the mold and its contents. Place platter over mold and invert. Rap on bottom of mold and perhaps shake once sideways. You can hear and almost feel the slurping sound of release. Unmold completely and garnish according to the ingredients of the mousse. For example, a purée of salmon piped into a mousseline or puréed mixture of scallops appears to be a yolk surrounded by the white when presented in small ramekins. Place these molds on pillows of blanched fresh spinach. A bit of cooked scallop purée on top, or a smoked scallop, or a chunk of smoked salmon, would be a clue to the ingredients of the dish as well as a tasty flavor counterpoint. A cucumber mousse may have thin slices of bevelled cucumbers ringed around the mold between succulent pink whole shrimp. Rosettes of cream cheese whipped with a little mayonnaise last longer than plain mayonnaise or yogurt.

Savory Mousses, Aspics, and Gelatins

Many culinary books and resources have mousse, aspic, and gelatin recipes to experiment with and try on food friends first. Clear aspics especially may be adorned with vegetable flowers, black olive diamonds, and spades or hearts of any color bell peppers. Aloe vera gelatin is a healthy new alternative to gelatin made from animal products.

Little is more eye-catching than a fancy molded savoury or dessert or a rich pâté en croûte decorated with braids of bread dough or pastry and flowers. Simply turn out fruit gelatins from oiled molds. Present on oversized platters with plenty of room to garnish with appealingly cut fresh fruits, edible flowers, and whipped cream or a mix of ricotta and cream cheese, quark, or plain yogurt.

Eggs in aspic are a classic dish as is a turban of sole with an inner ring of shrimp mousse filling. Easier versions are simple layered vegetable flans puréed with cream and eggs baked like a custard. Center a colorful, large flan made in a charlotte mold or one-quart souffle dish in the hotel pan with one wedge severed. Surround the flan with individual soufflé ramekins or custard cups.

Save a few perfect vegetables to drop in the center of the mold or serve as a steamed garnish. Fresh mint is compatible with puréed peas; serve on a sturdy steam table bed of sautéed napa, savoy, or romaine mix. A chiffonade of basil for

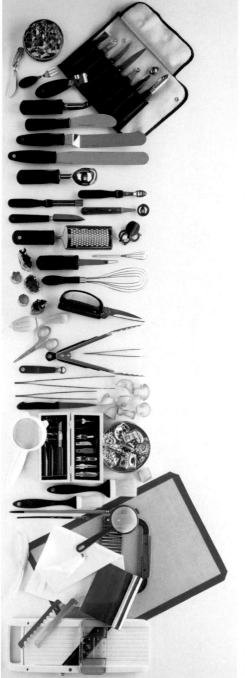

PLATE 1 (*top right*). Color wheel of fruits and vegetables, arranged by hue.

PLATE 2 (*left*). Garnishing tools, an overview. From top to bottom: top right, garde manger tool kit with citrus zester and decorator, bird's beak paring knife, 3" straight paring knife, mini vegetable scoop, double vegetable scoop, vegetable peeler; top left, variety of shaped stamps; small butter or pâté spreader; small "oxo" fork to pierce smaller foods; stripper/zester; peeler; three different shaped palette knives or flexible spatulas; ice cream scoop; fluted, oval, and round scoops; apple corer and fluting knife; small grater for nutmeg and hard cheeses; photographer's loupe for magnifying food photographs or small garnishes; baby balloon whisk; curved and serrated grapefruit knife; whisk; animal- and other-shaped vegetable cutters; poultry shears; citrus reamer; poultry scissors; tongs and tweezers; tomato topper or corer (with red handle); stamps (right of tweezers); X-ACTO carving set, 15 cutting blades and handle in wooden box; nylon mesh sieve for powdered sugar; pastry and egg wash brushes; camel's hair paint brushes; white feather for brushing; white pastry bag and fluted tip; smooth and scalloped pastry cutters or bench scrapers; Silpat nonstick baking mat (beneath pastry cutters) for working sugar, chocolate, etc.; Beni vegetable slicer with various blades.

PLATE 3 (*bottom right*). Garnish layouts, samples, and lemon basket with herbs.

PLATE 4 (*top*). Cold cut platters, cold meats and cheeses, cheese board.
PLATE 5 (*above left*). Chicken wings and drummettes and dipping sauces.
PLATE 6 (*above right*). Egg rolls, potstickers, sushi, wasabi, and pickled ginger.

PLATE 7 (*above*). Salad samplers: Wild Waldorf, Antipasto Chop-Chop Salad, Golden Lemon Lentil, Chilled Jambalaya.

PLATE 8 (*left*). Cheeses, fruits, and crackers.

PLATE 15 (*left*). Crockpot salads surrounded with bread.
PLATE 16 (*below*). Cold pasta bar.

PLATE 17 (*top*). Brunch at Bally's, Las Vegas.
PLATE 18 (*right*). Scrambled eggs in avocados, puff pastry, chayote, phyllo cups, and acorn squashes, all arranged in a chafing dish.

PLATE 19 (*top left*). Breakfast breads and fresh fruit on platters with granola in a decorative glass jar.

PLATE 20 (top *right*). Broiled breakfast sandwiches, torta, bagels, and accoutrements.

PLATE 21 (*left*). Egg, spinach, and phyllo strata with pepper baskets of herbs.

PLATE 22 (*top left*).   Macadamia banana–stuffed French toast with cream cheese and jam, berries, and powdered sugar.
PLATE 23 (top right).   Potato latkes with zucchini and golden squash, topped with applesauce and sour cream.
PLATE 24 (*right*).   Juice bar.

PLATE 25. Wok cooking demonstration.

PLATE 26 (*top*). Trout fillets on rice pilaf with Sauce Veronique.
PLATE 27 (*above*). Seafood casserole served in individual seashells set on rock salt in a hotel pan.

PLATE 28 (*top*). Fish fillets en papillote on bed of lemon-lime rice in a pink chafing dish.
PLATE 29 (*above*). Chicken in a chafing pan with roasted vegetables.

PLATE 30 (*top*). Sliced beef with chrysanthemum potatoes and onions.
PLATE 31 (*above*). Pasta, rice, and grains, in various shapes and colors.

PLATE 32. The Renaissance Courtyard in bloom: a formal catering buffet.

eggplant or tomato works well sprinkled over timbales just before service. Aluminum dariole molds are ideal for gelatins and savarins, babas au rhum, and other miniature bread loaves.

Why stop at mousses and gelatins? A savory rice timbale filled with seafood mousse makes a sturdy steam table entrée. Cut a large timbale into wedges using an eight-wedge pie marker. Rice mixtures are fine served hot, room temperature, or cold. Vary flavor, texture, and ethnic orientation by adding raisins, almonds, herbs of choice (no more than three or they fight for attention), green peas, saffron, a little wild rice, Kashi, spelt, basmati rice, curry, cumin, cinnamon, and allspice with mushrooms and peppers for a Mideastern flavor profile. Decorate the inside of the mold with stamped vegetable flowers, pepper triangles or hearts, olive halves, onion patterns, or whatever suits your time and budget constraints.

Different dishes from the same mold, different textures and shapes of foods with entirely different decorative embellishments and colors have highly individual personalities. No matter how beautifully presented or delicious the finished dishes are, if the foods on your tray or steam table all have the same texture, appearance, and decoration, they make a boring meal, line, or platter.

✱ AVOCADO MOUSSE WITH CRAB LOUIS DRESSING

YIELD: 1 quart

INGREDIENTS

AVOCADO MOUSSE

1 package Knox unflavored gelatin	$^1/_2$ cup nonfat ricotta
$^1/_2$ cup dry white wine	4 avocados, large and ripe
$^1/_2$ cup chicken broth, heated	2 teaspoons onion, grated
2 tablespoons lemon juice	2 dashes Tabasco
$^1/_2$ cup quark or nonfat sour cream	

GARNISH

1 pound crab or shrimp	Parsley or watercress sprigs

(Continued)

CRAB LOUIS DRESSING

$^1/_2$ cup quark

$^1/_2$ cup plain yogurt

$^1/_4$ cup chili sauce

2 tablespoons sweet pickle relish

2 tablespoons sherry or white wine

1 tablespoon onion, minced

1 tablespoon celery, minced

1 teaspoon capers

1 teaspoon lemon juice

$^1/_2$ teaspoon Worcestershire sauce

$^1/_8$ teaspoon pepper, freshly ground

INSTRUCTIONS

Soften gelatin in wine for 5 minutes, then dissolve mixture in heated chicken broth. Add lemon juice and cool thoroughly. Peel avocados and puree. Add onion and Tabasco to avocados, then fold quark and ricotta into broth mixture. Pour into oiled or sprayed 1- to $1^1/_2$-quart ring mold or bundt pan. Chill several hours or overnight.

Mix dressing ingredients well and chill.

Garnish unmolded mousse with parsley or watercress and little mounds of crab or shrimp. Serve Louis dressing on the side in a fancy dish with a ladle for guests to pour their own.

For a south-of-the-border change of pace, use seviche as a topping for the mousse.

BLOODY MARY MOUSSE WITH OLD BAY SEAFOOD

YIELD: 12 servings

INGREDIENTS

2 packages Knox unflavored gelatin

$^1/_2$ cup water or vodka

2 cups spicy tomato juice or Bloody Mary mix

1 cup V8 juice or water

1 tablespoon dill, minced

$^1/_2$ cup (2 oz) onion, minced

$^1/_2$ cup (4 oz) celery, minced

$^1/_2$ cup (4 oz) green pepper, minced

DRESSING/SEAFOOD MIX

1 cup light mayonnaise

8 oz nonfat cream cheese

1 pound crab (surimi) or shrimp,
   cooked, diced

1–2 teaspoons Old Bay seasoning
   (or to taste)

2 teaspoons lemon juice, fresh

$1/2$ tablespoon chives, freeze-dried

Salt and freshly ground pepper to taste

GARNISHES

Parsley or watercress sprigs

Lemon and lime wedges or wheels

INSTRUCTIONS

Soften gelatin in water for 5 minutes. Heat spicy tomato juice, V8 juice, dill, onion, celery, and green pepper. Stir in gelatin mixture and dissolve. Remove from heat and cool. In the meantime, mix dressing ingredients. Pour gelatin into lightly sprayed molds. Serve dressing on the side or pour a little over the mousse. Wrap and chill.

Unmold onto oversize platters, unless you made individual molds. Garnish with parsley and citrus wheels at will. Place whole shrimp in pockets in the mold.

DRESSINGS

The dressing portion of a salad bar is an arena of creative opportunity. Not only can you present signature dressings, but the bottles and vessels themselves make great props. Bottles of vinegar and oils with unique herbs and flavorings make a lovely display on a back shelf or on the ice bed itself.

If the salad dressings are particularly healthful and salable, package them for retail sales or as an add-on feature of platters to go. You can find small jars at antique stores or import shops or use empty wine bottles for your special dressing or vinegar. The packaging can be made quite pretty with the addition of colored wax and ribbons, bright labels with calligraphy, and recipes utilizing the product.

Fresh fruit vinegars are a bright, flavorful addition to your salad bar and to specific dressings. A line up of kiwi–green apple, apricot peach, and plum huckleberry vinegar will enliven any display.

Ideal stuffings for flavored vinegars include:

- A garden sampler of oregano, rosemary, shallots, garlic, and pear tomato
- Edible flowers, including borage, chive blossoms, and flowering thyme or oregano
- Spicy Southwestern notes—chile peppers, cilantro, garlic, and red pepper flakes
- Tropical elements—starfruit, mint, mango and pomegranate seeds
- An English garden variation of Ditmus-on-thyme (or lemon thyme)

The classic international and regional dressing formulas should be available but do feature some of your own. Italian vinaigrette with balsamic vinegar, French dressing, and house vinaigrette are always popular. However, you can try a Mediterranean lemon herbed vinaigrette or Mexican cilantro pepita dressing for a nice change.

These salad dressings have proven track records.

★ QUICK-CHANGE LEMON BALSAMIC VINAIGRETTE

So easy and so much better than commercial versions, this dressing also has menu overlap possibilities. Use as a dressing or marination with three different flavor profiles.

YIELD: $3^{1}/_{4}$ cups

INGREDIENTS

$^{1}/_{4}$ cup Country Dijon or Pommery mustard

2 tablespoons kosher salt

1 tablespoon freshly ground pepper

2 teaspoons garlic, minced or roasted and puréed

$^{1}/_{4}$ cup basil cut to chiffonade

$^{1}/_{4}$ cup parsley, minced

1 tablespoon plus 2 teaspoons rosemary, minced

$^{1}/_{4}$ cup balsamic vinegar

1 cup lemon juice

$1^{2}/_{3}$ cups extra-virgin olive oil

INSTRUCTIONS

Whisk mustard, salt, pepper, garlic, basil, parsley, rosemary, and vinegar. Allow the vinegar to dissolve the salt. Whisk in lemon juice and oil. Place in covered container; label, date, rotate, and refrigerate.

✳ *ADD-IN VARIATIONS*

Sun-Dried Tomato Pesto: Mix 2:1 dressing to pesto.
Kalamata Olive Vinaigrette: Mix 2:1 to chopped olives.
Pesto Lemon Vinaigrette: Mix 2:1 to basil pesto.

✳ LOW-FAT LOUIS DRESSING

YIELD: about 9 cups

INGREDIENTS

2 cups light or nonfat mayonnaise

2 cups plain nonfat yogurt

1 cup light or nonfat sour cream

1 cup chili sauce

1 tablespoon plus 1 teaspoon reduced-calorie Worcestershire sauce

4 garlic cloves, minced or roasted and puréed

4 dashes cayenne or hot pepper sauce

$1/2$ cup lemon juice

1 cup green pepper, minced

1 cup green onion, sliced thinly

INSTRUCTIONS

In a large bowl, combine all ingredients. Taste and reseason if necessary. Place dressing in covered container; label, date, rotate, and refrigerate.

✳ LOW-CALORIE FRESH LEMON VINAIGRETTE

YIELD: 1 quart plus 1 pint

INGREDIENTS

$^1/_4$ cup Pommery or Country Dijon mustard

1–2 tablespoons kosher or sea salt

$^3/_4$ teaspoon freshly ground black pepper

8–10 cloves garlic, minced or roasted and puréed

$^1/_4$ cup basil, cut to chiffonade

$^1/_4$ cup parsley, minced

2 tablespoons rosemary, minced

1–3 teaspoons red pepper flakes

3 tablespoons lemon rind, grated or zested

1 pint lemon juice

$^1/_2$ cup balsamic vinegar

6 ounces or $^2/_3$ cup walnut, olive, or safflower oil

1 quart vegetarian chicken broth

INSTRUCTIONS

Whisk mustard, salt, pepper, garlic, basil, parsley, rosemary, red pepper flakes, lemon rind, lemon juice, and vinegar. Allow the vinegar to dissolve the salt. Whisk in lemon juice and oil. Place dressing in covered container; label, date, rotate, and refrigerate.

✳ PACIFIC RIM GINGER SESAME DRESSING

First developed for a seafood magazine this dressing also worked well in a salad bar and passed the tight standards of a professional taste panel.

YIELD: $2^2/_3$ cups

INGREDIENTS

3 tablespoons fresh ginger, peeled and coarsely chopped

3 cloves garlic, minced or roasted and puréed

1 tablespoon orange zest

1 tablespoon red pepper flakes

$^1/_4$ cup mint, chopped

$^1/_4$ cup cilantro, chopped

$^1/_2$ cup honey

$^1/_3$ cup tamari, shoyu, Bragg's, or light soy sauce

3 tablespoons sesame seeds, black and white

$^1/_3$ cup oriental dark sesame oil

$^1/_2$ cup peanut or light salad oil

INSTRUCTIONS

Combine ginger, garlic, orange zest, red pepper flakes, mint, cilantro, honey, tamari, and sesame seeds in blender. Blend. While machine is running, gradually add sesame and peanut oils, blending until smooth. Place in covered container; label, date, rotate, and refrigerate.

✦ MANGO LIME DRESSING

This goes well with an artichoke and goat cheese salad.

YIELD: 3 pints

INGREDIENTS

1 cup chutney, chopped finely

1 cup plain nonfat yogurt

1 cup nonfat cream cheese

1 cup balsamic vinegar

9 fresh mangoes, peeled and sliced

INSTRUCTIONS

Purée all ingredients in processor or blender. Place dressing in covered container; label, date, rotate, and refrigerate.

✳ CREAMY FRUITY SPELT TABOULI DRESSING

This is great for any fruit or Waldorf salad or fruit cream parfait.

YIELD: 5 cups

INGREDIENTS

1 tablespoon orange zest

1 tablespoon tangerine zest

$^2/_3$ cup lemon juice

$^1/_4$ cup orange juice

2 tablespoons Dijon or Pommery
   mustard

1 cup mint, roughly chopped

1 cup parsley, roughly chopped

1 teaspoon cinnamon

$^1/_2$ teaspoon ground cumin

$^1/_4$ teaspoon fresh grated nutmeg

12 ounces nonfat quark, whipped

$^1/_2$ cup canola oil

$^1/_2$ cup olive oil

INSTRUCTIONS

Combine all ingredients. Place dressing in covered container; label, date, rotate, and refrigerate.

SPICY AVOCADO SALAD DRESSING

I have created variations of this dressing for restaurant chains, cookbooks, and councils and farmers' cooperatives.

YIELD: 4 cups

INGREDIENTS

2 cups plain nonfat yogurt

2 avocados, peeled, seeded, and coarsely chopped

$^2/_3$ cup lemon juice or orange juice

$^1/_4$ cup lime juice

2 cloves garlic, crushed or minced

1 teaspoon salt

$^1/_2$ teaspoon hot pepper sauce

$^1/_2$ teaspoon ground cumin or chili powder

INSTRUCTIONS

Combine all ingredients in a food processor; blend until smooth and well mixed. Place dressing in covered container; label, date, rotate, and refrigerate.

BREAKFAST BUFFETS AND LINES

5

Breakfast buffets begin at a simple level—breakfast-on-the run quick meals, trays to go, and an almost infinite number of meal-in-the-hand options. At the other end of the spectrum are the elaborate hotel and resort brunches with cascading fruits, waterfalls of champagne, and chefs preparing omelets, crepes, and sweet flambéed desserts before the eyes of the guests. Somewhere in between are many other levels of food service. All can benefit from creative garnishing and artful arranging (see Color Plate 17).

The way a brunch buffet or tray is presented plays a vital role in how well it is accepted and perceived as a good value by guests. The more bountiful, colorful, and fresh it looks, the more diners believe they chose the right place to enjoy Saturday or Sunday brunch. A variety of foods, colorful decorations, and an attentive staff all lend themselves to an experience guests will long remember and tell their friends about. Each food station and category must maintain its appeal throughout the brunch; to-go trays must be equally attractive.

Provide chilled crocks full of toppings and fillings at egg and omelet bars. Replace decorative vegetables and kale as needed and clean up spills promptly.

Make scrambled eggs with a roux; they hold up longer in chafing dishes. Constantly monitor cleanliness, the key to any successful meal.

Waffle bars must provide full and clean containers of syrups, spreads, and condiments. Garnishes should be replaced as needed for freshness. All rims of trays should be spotless unless sauce art or dusted minced herbs are part of the final presentation.

Hot cereals and breakfast potatoes should be served hot. These two mostly white dishes can be a canvas for multicolored garnishes, including black or golden raisins, toasted coconut, nuts, minced fresh herbs, edible petals, sliced green onion, dollops of sour cream, thunderbolts of salsa roja and verde from a squeeze bottle, and all the produce garnishes categorized by color in Chapter 1.

Breakfast fruit soups and shakes are colorful on their own but benefit from a simple sprig of mint or citrus wheel. An entire bed of ice is a ready-made backdrop for whole and cut fruits, fluted melons for soups, and a variety of shake blends.

Breakfast sandwiches work best for meal-in-the-hand options, fast breakfast meetings, or to-go deli trays. Simply toast two pieces of bread and fill with fruit butters, sliced meats, cheeses, vegetable combinations, or sausage. Wrap in foil for out-of-hand eating.

Tortillas, chalupas, and other wraps can embrace many fillings for quick and easy to-go service. The presentation may be rolled as a flauta or enchilada, small or large, folded as a burrito, or layered as a torta and cut to wedges. Stratas and layered casseroles such as chilaquiles are easy to cut and serve in squares, triangles, or individual casserole or ramekin dishes.

On all exhibition stations, keep linen, utensils, and serving dishes in good condition; clean and replace as needed. Keep the surrounding floor clean and swept and wash up all spills promptly. Staff uniforms should be just as clean and crisp as the linens. Proper and ample lighting is also important; it lends warmth to buffet displays and enhances the look of freshness and quality.

As important as the appearance of the buffet are the condition and temperature of the food. The following methods of keeping hot food hot and fresh work for brunch, lunch, or dinner, hot line service, and demonstration carts.

Serving hot food hot (150°F) requires the right equipment, pan size and rotation, and food runners. Dedicate an employee to the task of running food in order to maintain the freshness and correct serving temperature of the hot foods. Food services with high brunch counts need at least two food runners during the peak periods. For to-go trays, simply write specific heating instructions and describe garnishes for the platter that the client may easily manage at home.

The two types of equipment used to present hot foods are chafing dishes or hotel pans and hot carts. Chafing dishes are electric or heated by Sterno. Hot carts are electrical. In all cases, water is heated to generate steam, which in turn heats the food gently from the bottom. Some hot carts have the capability to heat food from the top through the use of heat lamps, which should be clear and kept clean for maximum efficiency. Equipment should always be in top working order. Maintain water levels and, if using Sterno, replace it as needed throughout the brunch so that the heat source is constant. Develop a Sterno replacement schedule based on the length of time a canister lasts. You might even replace a canister before it is completely empty to ensure that food stays hot.

Have the right amount of food on display based on the volume of guests. Pan size and rotation is the key to maintaining hot, fresh foods. You can vary the amount of food through the use of different sizes of hotel pans. Full-size, half-size, third-pans, and long half-size or alley pans are all available. Put out the least amount of food required to ensure that the food is rotated regularly, that it is always hot and fresh, and that the pan is full—this conveys the sense of bounty to the guests.

Two types of half-size pans are available. A regular half-size pan is filled with food, while an empty half-size pan, with lid, occupies the space behind it in the chafing dish or hot cart. This presentation is suitable for slow periods and makes it easy to transfer into full size pans when volume increases. Pans are generally $2\frac{1}{2}$–4 inches deep.

The other type of half-size pan is the long half or alley pan. This allows you to make food accessible to guests from two sides if your setup is designed for it. As with regular half-size pans, foods can be transferred to full-size pans when volume picks up.

Managing pans is a constant responsibility throughout brunch. Guest flow through the front door must be monitored at all times to ensure that you are using the right pans for the amount of business. You might decide to serve a slow-moving food in a half pan for the entire brunch. The prep sheet helps in determining each food's usage during an average brunch, which in turn helps you to choose the correct pan size. Using half pans also increases the number of products you can offer in a standard eight pan steam table.

Another key to presentation is keeping pans clean. This means that the food runner may need to re-pan food periodically in order to maintain the display's fresh look. Fresh full pans should be brought to the chafing dishes or hot carts to replace pans that are empty or have lost their appeal. Old food should not be transferred to the new pans in the view of the guests. Re-panning should occur in the kitchen only. Take old pans to the kitchen for the chef to re-pan, stock, and garnish. You might need to build up your inventory of half-size pans and purchase some long half-size pans for your brunch. Have enough pans on hand so that you can always have a backup for each hot food item ready to go in a clean pan. When you practice proper pan usage and rotation, hot foods look fresh and stay hot from beginning to end.

Communication between the manager, the chef, and the food runners is vital to the correct panning of food for the anticipated business. Proper training of the food runner goes a long way toward ensuring hot, fresh foods throughout brunch. Managing pan sizes is the responsibility of the manager or chef, but the food runner and cooks must stay alert and follow instructions in order to maintain quality.

The simplest way to train runners in the standards of excellence in hot food presentation is to set up your hot foods prior to opening in a fresh, full, and appealing manner. Bring your food runner to the chafing dishes and hot carts to show how the food looks. Explain that it should look like that for the entire brunch or meal service and that this is achieved by rotating pans of food and wiping spills promptly.

A food runner should not be afraid to call for help when needed and a second food runner (or more) must be scheduled for peak periods at high-volume restaurants. A food runner must anticipate the business and be alert to diminishing foods. Cooks must prepare and pan food before the displayed pans run out so guests are not left waiting. During peak periods, certain foods may be prepared, panned, and held in a warming cabinet to help in maintaining availability. When a food runner calls for food, the cooks should react immediately so that the guest flow around the hot foods is not disrupted by outages. An alert staff working as a team can maintain the flawless presentation of fresh, hot, and appealing foods.

Bally's Hotel in Las Vegas has one of the most elegant and opulent brunches anywhere. Chef de cuisine Todd Clore runs a small army of chefs to put on this $50-per-person extravaganza. These professionals pride themselves on the complete edibility of every garnish and decoration. The 13 garde-manger chefs design beautiful watermelon flowers and melon petals resting inside of one another. Even the tortellini pasta is hand-shaped to resemble rosebuds. Ice carvings form vases or cornucopias with carved vegetable flowers.

Chef Clore declares that, besides the flawless embellishments and high-end props, one of the biggest challenges is keeping hot food hot and cold food cold; for example, he had a 12-inch-deep Plexiglas ice bath custom built for the cold table. This ice bed takes 750 pounds of ice.

The hot side of the buffet displays beautiful round sterling and silver chafing dishes that can hold only seven portions. Chef Clore prefers a Heat-It wick to Sterno because the wick gets closer to the pan and heats it higher and longer than the open flame. The chafers are only 2½ inches deep, so food must be replaced quickly and frequently. In fact, it takes five food runners to keep this buffet looking splendid.

Other brunch employees include five hot line servers, two sushi chefs, four pastry chefs, and one person each at the dessert demonstration area, the carving area, the waffle station, and the omelette station.

Serving hot food hot is an important element in keeping and building brunch counts and sales. The freshness and flavor of your foods are greatly enhanced when they are properly prepared and presented. Your efforts to maintain the beauty of your foods through the talents and teamwork of your employees will yield the satisfaction your guests expect. Being alert and aware at all times ensures that you consistently live up to their expectations.

Here's a sample menu for easy, healthy breakfast options.

BREAKFAST OPTIONS

Fast and Fresh

1$\frac{1}{2}$ cups whole-grain cereal
8 ounces skim soy milk (2% fat)

2 nonfat Eggo Special K waffles
1 cup nonfat sugar-free yogurt

$\frac{1}{2}$ cup oatmeal with
   1 tablespoon fructose

1 slice whole-wheat toast
2 teaspoons peanut butter
8 ounces orange juice

1 bagel with nonfat cream cheese
1 tablespoon unsweetened jam
$\frac{1}{2}$ cup unsweetened applesauce

3 regular or sourdough pancakes
2 tablespoons maple syrup
6 ounces orange juice

2 slices whole-grain toast
2 ounces low-fat cheese of choice
8 ounces mixed fresh orange
  and grapefruit juices

Creative Additions and Alternatives

Slice kiwi, peaches, apples, and bananas over cereal. Scatter berries and just a few nuts for crunch.

Substitute multigrain waffles, cooked and frozen. Add fresh fruit compote with 1 tablespoon maple syrup.

Substitute Scottish oatmeal or other whole-grain cooked cereals. Sprinkle frozen or fresh berries, turbinado or brown sugar, and cinnamon over cereal.

Substitute 1 slice homemade whole-grain bread. Use freshly ground peanut butter; add sliced bananas. Try an 8 ounce fast fruit shake.

Add raspberries to the applesauce.

Substitute buckwheat or whole-grain pancakes with $\frac{1}{4}$ cup hot fruit compote. Serve fruit juice blend instead of orange juice.

Try nonfat cottage cheese on toast. Add orange or pineapple segments and wheat germ.

Fruit nog (see recipe on p. 158)	Substitute a fast fruit frappe.
Fresh fruit soup	Serve breakfast fruit salad in melon
Broiled breakfast sandwich	bowls. Make the sandwich
Orange Banana Cream (see recipe on p. 159)	vegetarian.
Breakfast panacea quesadilla	Try Mexicali Scrambled Eggs with
Vegetarian variations	secret sauce. Serve with
Fast fruit shake	Wolferman English muffins.
Dutch Baby Puff Pancakes	Substitute Scandinavian puff
Fruit filling	pancakes. Use several fruits in
Fresh steamed asparagus	the filling.
Blueberry banana shake	
Breakfast pizza	Substitute Southwest breakfast
Coffee	pizza and café latte

EGG COOKERY

The principles of egg preparation are often overlooked in cookbooks and food service kitchens, yet what I learned about them at Cordon Bleu and tested at *Sunset* magazine has proven invaluable time and again. They are so important that I use them as a measuring stick of the cook's skill whenever I'm reviewing a restaurant or gauging the quality of its cuisine. One of the keys is not to boil eggs but to gently simmer them to avoid the horrid green sulfur ring, denatured protein, and tough taste. Coddling eggs and poaching them gently for a tender mouth-feel is tricky but essential.

Eggs can be prepared quickly and project aesthetic appeal with the use of imaginative techniques, fillings, toppings, and sauces. Heat-and-hold scrambled, baked, and poached eggs hold up better along a steam table than do scrambled or fried eggs. A colorful egg scramble can be presented in an acorn squash or nestled inside a hollowed chayote or zucchini boat. Design a mold shaped like a bowtie and cook over-easy or poached eggs in it for a whimsical presentation. The shredded potato nest is a classic edible container too (see Color Plate 18).

All kinds of additions may be added to baked eggs, including steamed asparagus tips, sautéed mushrooms, tomato bits, and creamed spinach. For increased protein, heartiness, and price, top with diced bacon, chicken hash, julienned smoked turkey, sausage, or even anchovy. For crunch, place a round of any toasted Pullman loaf slice in the bottom of the baking dish and top with Gruyère or any other cheese. Add fresh eggs and bake at 350°F for 6–7 minutes au bain-marie with poaching paper on top.

Omelets and frittatas are better than baked eggs, of course, for interactive quick service. Demonstrate the procedure from a two-burner gas flame with backup cartridge. Present an array of crocks with fillings and toppings resting in an ice bath.

Stratas, chilaquiles, and egg enchiladas or flautas work well for steam table service too. Try coloring the eggs green for St. Patrick's Day or decorating them with heart shapes cut out of red bell peppers at St. Valentine's Day. Colorful minced peppers, confetti of diced edible flowers, or root vegetables stamped to shapes and steamed make an amusing bright garnish. Of course, scallion fans and citrus wheels are always attractive. Try an orange slice against a spray of sprouts to symbolize the rising sun.

✱ AVOCADO OMELET WITH BASQUE SAUCE

The sauce on this colorful omelet has a multiplicity of uses—potato stuffer, pasta sauce, and sauce for eggplant parmigiana and grilled chicken.

YIELD: 1 serving

INGREDIENTS

$1/4$ California avocado, halved, pitted, and peeled

3 eggs

1 tablespoon water

1 tablespoon butter

4 ounces Basque Sauce (see p. 132)

1 ounce Jack cheese, shredded (optional)

INSTRUCTIONS

Slice the avocado into 3 slices.

Heat a 7- or 8-inch omelet pan over medium-high heat. Beat eggs and water with a fork just until well blended. Add butter to heated pan. When butter foams, pour in the eggs. Stir slowly 3 times around, counterclockwise, with a fork. Allow eggs to cook for a few seconds. With a fork, draw cooked portion at edge toward center, tilting pan as necessary, so the uncooked portion will reach the hot pan surface and create a beautiful fan effect.

While the top is moist and creamy, add 2 ounces Basque Sauce, cheese, and sliced avocado; fold omelet in half with a spatula. Shake pan gently to release omelet. Slide omelet out or quickly invert with a flick of the wrist.

For a frittata, leave the omelet open-faced and run under a salamander or broiler until cheese is melted and bubbly.

Top with remaining sauce and a sprinkling of cheese, and garnish with parsley.

✱ BASQUE SAUCE

YIELD: 12 servings, 4 ounces each

INGREDIENTS

8 ounces red onions, chopped

4 ounces zucchini, halved and sliced

6 ounces green pepper, julienned

3 garlic cloves, minced

2–3 tablespoons olive oil

16 ounces canned whole plum
 tomatoes, drained

$^{1}/_{2}$ cup dry red wine

2–3 tablespoons basil, fresh
 chopped

1 tablespoon fresh oregano, minced

1–2 teaspoons paprika

$^{1}/_{4}$ cup pimiento strips

INSTRUCTIONS

Sauté onions, zucchini, green pepper, and garlic in oil. Add the remaining ingredients and simmer 15 minutes.

IDAHO POTATO NESTS WITH CHARD AND EGGS

This tasty dish may look like a long job, but it may be prepared in stages.

YIELD: 12 servings

INGREDIENTS

POTATO ONION NESTS

1 quart plus 1 pint Idaho
   potato, grated

6 ounces red onion, grated

2–3 teaspoons salt

vegetable oil

CREAMED CHARD OR SPINACH

4–6 ounces butter

8–9 ounces all-purpose flour

7–9 cups 2% milk or evaporated
   skim milk

2 cups Asiago, white Cheddar, or
   Romano cheese, grated

$^3/_4$ teaspoon dry mustard

$^1/_2$ teaspoon nutmeg, freshly grated

Salt and freshly ground pepper

3 bunches fresh Swiss chard, collard
   or dandelion greens, or spinach,
   or a combination of these

24 eggs

INSTRUCTIONS

POTATO ONION NESTS

Preheat oven to 450°F. Oil 12 1-cup ramekins or custard cups. Mix potato, onion, and salt together and divide the mixture among the ramekins. Press it into the sides and bottoms, forming cups about $^1/_2$ inch thick. Brush lightly with oil. Bake for 30–40 minutes or until lightly browned and crisp. Set aside on cooling rack.

(Continued)

CREAMED CHARD OR SPINACH

While potato cups are baking, melt butter in large heavy saucepan over medium heat. Tilt pan and stir in the flour; when the mixture begins to bubble, reduce heat to low and cook, whisking constantly, about 3 minutes. Gradually pour in the milk, still whisking, and simmer until thickened, about 5 minutes. Add the cheese and stir until melted. Stir in dry mustard, nutmeg, salt, and pepper, and add greens of choice. Remove pan from heat.

ASSEMBLY

Preheat broiler. Poach or lightly scramble the eggs in a little butter, leaving slightly underdone. Divide eggs among nests and cover with warm creamed spinach. Put ramekins under broiler for a minute or two, until surface is lightly browned. Serve immediately, if possible.

To prepare in advance, bake nests and cream spinach. At serving time, reheat spinach, cook eggs, and finish as above.

BREAKFAST BREADS

Breakfast quick breads are superb on their own for breakfasts eaten out of hand or as an addition to a full buffet. They also lend themselves to a variety of fillings and toppings and are both easy to pre-

At the Old Country Buffet in Spokane, Washington, eggs go quickly at each Saturday and Sunday brunch. Liquid egg substitutes are used for scrambled eggs, first on the grill and then in a holding oven at about 160° F. This ensures a nicer presentation and quality than holding does.

Half pans are used for the eggs to turn them over quickly. Serving spoons and props are monitored and replaced often as part of the constant attention to cleanliness. Two or three runners are used during the peak periods to monitor all the stations.

pare and aromatic. Look for tall bread loaf molds that shape batter into clovers, triangles, or flowers. Bread sliced from these loaves elevates the presentation.

Present platters of sliced variety breads and cut fresh fruit. Adding one or two exotic fruits offers a colorful conversation piece (see Color Plate 19). Creamed honey citrus butters and compound butter spreads are attractive, flavorful additions to breakfast breads. A scattering of berries or dollops of unsweetened jams or marmalades with whipped cream cheese are excellent touches. Bagels are easier to purchase than to bake yourself. Serve them with flavored butters and cream cheeses, lox, or any smoked fish (see Color Plate 20).

To reheat cornbread, split it and toast in broiler. Sprinkle with celery, poppy, or sesame seeds or spread with a little sweet or fruit butter. To reheat muffins, wrap them in foil, place on bottom rack of oven preheated to 300°F, and heat about 10 minutes. For scones, pour about a cup of water into a hotel pan and place on the bottom of a 200°F oven, under the racks. Place a rack in bottom rung of oven and arrange scones on it. Heat in 300°F oven for 5–10 minutes or until hot. The technique for reheating crusty (stale) French bread is to wrap it in a clean, damp tea towel. Set wrapped bread in a preheated 400°F oven for 10 minutes.

Nut and fruit loaves may be frozen for up to three months if tightly wrapped in foil or freezer wrap. When planning to freeze waffles or French toast, bake only until lightly browned. Cool completely on wire racks; wrap in foil or freezer wrap or freeze on sheet pans, place in heavy-duty plastic bags, and seal; freeze for one to two months. To thaw, simply remove from the package and toast in toaster.

For a pleasing change from syrup and jam toppings, try fresh chopped fruits and nuts, fruit butters, and flavored ricotta and Neufchâtel cheeses for a colorful, delicious, nutritious taste experience, less cloyingly sweet.

Muffins and other quick breads may be made ahead for breakfast or lunch. Biscuits, muffins, and scones brown best if baked on shiny metal cookie sheets and pans. For browning loaves, use loaf pans of dull metal, aluminum, or glass. Muffin pans should have $2\frac{1}{2}$-inch cups and be filled two-thirds full. After spooning batter into muffin cups, half fill any empty cups with water.

Unless the recipe directs otherwise, always stir dry ingredients together for even distribution but *don't overmix*. Batter will be lumpy, not smooth, and all ingredients should be just moistened. Overmixed breads and muffins are coarse-textured and tough, with tunnels throughout. Perfect muffins are tender, even-textured, and only slightly rounded on top. There are many variations once you master the culinary principles. Alternatively, find a great purveyor like Real Food Marketing Co., Inc.

✳ SAVORY MUFFINS

YIELD: 24 servings

INGREDIENTS

3 eggs

3 cups skim milk

$^1/_2$–$^3/_4$ cup safflower oil or butter

3 cups all-purpose flour

3 cups whole-wheat flour

$^1/_4$ cup brown sugar

$^1/_3$ cup wheat germ

2 teaspoons baking powder

$^1/_2$ teaspoon salt

1$^1/_2$ teaspoons baking soda

INSTRUCTIONS

Preheat oven to 400°F. Grease bottoms only 24 muffins cups. In a bowl, beat eggs, milk, and oil. In a separate bowl, stir together remaining ingredients; add to liquid mixture all at once. Mix just until dry ingredients are moistened. Batter will be lumpy. Fill muffin cups two-thirds full with batter. Bake 20–25 minutes or until golden brown. Turn muffins out of pan immediately.

✳ CEREAL MUFFINS

Decrease milk to 1$^1/_2$ cups. Omit all-purpose flour. Add 2 cups bran cereal, spelt, or corn flakes or oatmeal to batter.

✳ PEANUT BUTTER AND JELLY MUFFINS

Fill muffin cups half full with batter. Drop 1 teaspoon peanut butter and 1 teaspoon jelly into center of each. Add more batter until cups are two-thirds full.

✳ SWEET FRUIT MUFFINS

Stir into batter 3 cups of blueberries, raspberries, or cranberries, fresh or dried, and 1 tablespoon grated lemon peel or zest.

✳ *NUT-TOPPED MUFFINS*

Combine 1 cup brown sugar, some chopped nuts, and $1^1/_2$ teaspoons cinnamon or pumpkin pie spice. Sprinkle over batter in muffin cups.

✳ *APPLE SPICE MUFFINS*

Stir into batter 3 cups grated apple and $1^1/_2$ teaspoons cinnamon or pumpkin pie spice.

✳ OLD-FASHIONED SCONES

The variations below are ways to experiment with flavors and fillings. There are also many fine purveyors of scoop-and-bake scones and muffins. Ask your sales representative for samples.

YIELD: 16 servings

INGREDIENTS

6 cups all-purpose flour

2 tablespoons baking powder

$^3/_4$ teaspoon kosher, coarse, or sea salt

9 tablespoons unsalted butter

4 eggs, 2–3 tablespoons egg white reserved

1 cup evaporated skim milk

Sugar or Parmesan cheese, optional

INSTRUCTIONS

Preheat oven to 400°F.

In a large bowl, stir together flour, baking powder, and salt. Cut in butter until mixture resembles fine crumbs. Add eggs mixed with evaporated milk; mix until a stiff dough forms. Turn dough out onto a lightly floured board. Knead quickly until dough holds together. Divide dough in half. Pat each half into two 6-inch circles, each 1 inch thick. Cut each circle into quarters. Arrange quarters 1 inch apart on a large baking sheet. Brush tops with beaten reserved egg white. Sprinkle with sugar or grated Parmesan cheese, if desired. Bake for 15 minutes or until golden brown.

(Continued)

Scones are best served hot. The traditional accompaniments are Devonshire cream, sweet butter, marmalade, or any berry preserve.

✳ CHEESE SCONES

Add to dough $1^{1}/_{2}$ cups sharp white Cheddar cheese.

✳ ORANGE SCONES

Add to dough 3 tablespoons grated orange peel and $^{3}/_{4}$ teaspoon vanilla or 1 tablespoon Cointreau or Grand Marnier. Frost baked scones with powdered sugar and orange juice mixed to a spreading consistency. Fill each center with unsweetened berry jam, if desired.

✳ WHOLE-WHEAT AND HERB SCONES

Decrease flour by 2 cups. Make up with whole-wheat flour and add $1^{1}/_{2}$ cups fresh chopped herbs of your choice. One good combination is parsley, chives, and basil.

✳ RAISIN CITRUS SCONES

Add $1^{1}/_{2}$ cup sultanas, raisins, or currants and zest of lemon, lime, and orange. Walnuts are an optional source of crunch.

✳ WHOLE-WHEAT HEALTH PANCAKES

These pancakes are great served with a fruit purée or flavored ricotta, quark, or cream cheese spread. They can also be served with yogurt and sliced strawberries or syrup or honey flavored with Grand Marnier and grated orange and lemon peel.

YIELD: 24 pancakes, 4 inches in diameter

INGREDIENTS

2 cups all-purpose flour

$^1/_2$ cup whole-wheat pastry flour

$^1/_4$ cup stoneground cornmeal

$^1/_4$ cup wheat germ

2 tablespoons baking powder

2 teaspoons baking soda

$^1/_2$ teaspoon kosher or sea salt

4 eggs, lightly beaten

2 cups plain nonfat yogurt

2 cups skim milk

2 tablespoons safflower oil

2 tablespoons honey

Canola oil or light oil as needed

GARNISHES

Fluted melon

Berries

Citrus peel or zest (optional)

INSTRUCTIONS

In a mixing bowl, stir together all-purpose flour, whole-wheat flour, cornmeal, wheat germ, baking powder, baking soda, and salt. Add eggs, yogurt, milk, safflower oil, and honey; stir vigorously until smooth, or use a small mixer.

Heat a little canola or light oil in large skillet or on griddle over medium-high heat. Cook pancakes by quarter cupfuls until golden brown on both sides.

Overlap cakes in chafer or hotel pan. Center a fluted cantaloupe or honeydew between pancakes. Scatter berries and citrus zest over all.

✳ SPELT PANCAKES

Omit all-purpose flour and replace with spelt flour. Replace skim milk with 1 cup organic apple juice and 1 cup soy milk. Replace 2 eggs with 2 egg whites only. Fold 1 cup blueberries into batter. Serve with diced apples, mangoes, bananas, and pears.

★ COTTAGE CHEESE PANCAKES

This light and fluffy pancake has a citrus aroma and is very flavorful. Garnish with sliced oranges, strawberries, bananas, plain or flavored yogurt, and nuts.

YIELD: 12 servings, 2 pancakes each

INGREDIENTS

2 eggs, beaten

2 egg whites, beaten

2 cups nonfat cottage cheese

2 cups plain nonfat yogurt

2 teaspoons vanilla extract

2 teaspoons grated orange rind

2 teaspoons grated lemon rind

1 cup whole-wheat flour

1 cup all-purpose flour

$1/4$ cup brown sugar

$1/2$ teaspoon sea salt

Cooking oil (as needed)

INSTRUCTIONS

Combine eggs with cottage cheese, plain nonfat yogurt, vanilla, and citrus zest. Mix flours, brown sugar, and salt. Combine wet and dry ingredients, stirring gently. Heat oil on griddle on medium-high heat. Use 2-ounce ladle or scoop to pour batter on griddle. Griddle to 24 pancakes.

STRATAS

Bed-and-breakfasts and small inns all over the country, as well as in Europe, are raising breakfasts to a leisurely epicurean encounter. In splendid surroundings, with grand views and wonderful table appointments, breakfast at a bed-and-breakfast is a new art form. Most breakfast formulas are tailored so that they can be prepared quickly with a minimum of service. These establishments do not have fully equipped food service kitchens, nor do they have wait staffs. Thus, their culinary concepts work well for quick breakfast buffets.

THE BASIC BREAKFAST STRATA

Here is a famous strata variation from The Rutherford House, a bed and breakfast in Brisbane, Australia.

YIELD: 8 servings

INGREDIENTS

1 pint milk, 2% or nonfat

$^1/_2$ cup vermouth

1–2 teaspoons dry mustard

$^1/_2$–1 teaspoon white pepper, freshly ground

2 1-pound loaves French or Italian bread, stale

2 tablespoons olive oil

$^1/_2$ cup basil, cut to chiffonade

6–8 roma tomatoes, sliced

1 pound nonfat herbed whipped cream cheese, 1 pound whipped smoked salmon cream cheese, or 1 pound nonfat cottage cheese plus 4 ounces reduced-fat Cheddar, shredded

4 eggs (or egg substitute), beaten

6 egg whites, whisked

1 cup evaporated skim milk or whipping cream

INSTRUCTIONS

On the day before service, combine milk, vermouth, dry mustard, and pepper in a large bowl. Dice the bread into $^1/_2$-inch squares and dip a few at a time in milk mixture. Remove bread and gently squeeze out as much liquid as possible, trying not to tear bread in the process.

Cover the bottom of an oval gratin dish or half hotel pan with olive oil and a single layer of bread slices. Place some of the basil, tomato slices, and cream cheese on top of the bread. Continue layering until all these ingredients are used. Pour the beaten eggs and egg whites over the top and cover with plastic wrap. Refrigerate overnight.

The following morning, remove from refrigerator 30 minutes before baking. Preheat oven to 350°F. Pour milk or whipping cream over the dish, covering evenly, and bake for 50–60 minutes or until top is golden brown.

✶ EGG AND SPINACH STRATA

For an easier but still lovely version of a strata, try this layered dish from Kris McIlvenna of the Greenbriar Inn and catering firm in Coeur d'Alene, Idaho (see Color Plate 21).

YIELD: 10 servings

INGREDIENTS

9 eggs

1 teaspoon nutmeg, freshly grated

12 phyllo leaves

$^1/_2$ cup unsalted butter, melted

1 pint cottage cheese, creamed

6 ounces feta cheese

20 ounces frozen spinach, thawed

GARNISHES

Tomatoes, sliced

Red onion rings

Roasted red peppers, wedged

California avocado slices

Watercress sprigs

INSTRUCTIONS

Preheat oven to 350°F. In a Hobart mixer, beat eggs and nutmeg on high for 3 minutes. In a well-buttered 9 × 13 baking dish place 4 individually buttered phyllo leaves. Pour half the egg mixture over them. In a skillet over high heat, reduce water from thawed spinach. Place half of the cottage cheese, feta, and spinach in egg mixture. Place 4 more individually buttered phyllo leaves on top. Add remaining egg mixture, cottage cheese, feta cheese, and spinach. Place last 4 individually buttered phyllo leaves on top. Bake for 45 minutes or until knife inserted in center comes out clean.

Cut in triangles or squares and serve with sliced tomatoes, red onion rings, or roasted red pepper and watercress sprigs and California avocado slices.

MORE BREAD DISHES

✳ WHITE FLOUR TORTILLAS (TORTILLAS DE HARINA)

I love to heat a plain tortilla with exciting fillings for a quick breakfast snack. Handmade tortillas are easy to make and much tastier than commercial varieties. Preparing them in an exhibition kitchen is good theater.

YIELD: 24 6-inch tortillas

INGREDIENTS

4 cups all-purpose, unbleached flour

1–2 teaspoons salt

1 teaspoon baking power

4 tablespoons shortening or lard

$1\frac{1}{2}$ cups warm water, approximately

INSTRUCTIONS

Combine flour, salt, and baking powder in a medium-size mixing bowl; cut in shortening. Make a well in center of mixture. Add water, a small amount at a time, and work mixture into a dough. Knead dough until smooth, cover, and set aside for 10 minutes. Form dough into 24 small balls the size of eggs. Roll each ball into a circle 6 inches in diameter. Heat a griddle or skillet over medium-high heat. Cook tortillas, one at a time, for about 1 minute on each side. Tortillas should be lightly speckled.

✳ CORN TORTILLAS (TORTILLAS DE MAIZ)

I spent my adolescent years in Santa Ana, California, and our next-door neighbors were wonderful Mexican cooks. The matriarch made these fresh tortillas every other day. I was instantly fascinated with both the process and the flavor. Like flour tortillas, corn tortillas make for a great show time exhibition station or kitchen.

YIELD: 12–14 6-inch tortillas

INGREDIENTS

2 cups blue or yellow masa harina $1^2/_3$ cups boiling water

$^1/_2$–1 teaspoon salt

INSTRUCTIONS

Combine masa harina and salt in a medium bowl. Add boiling water and stir until dough resembles thick cooked cereal. Wet hands and form dough into balls the size of an egg. Place each ball of dough between two lightly moistened pieces of waxed paper and flatten to about $^1/_8$-inch thick using a tortilla press, rolling pin, or pressure from the hands. Remove tortillas from waxed paper.

    Heat griddle or skillet over medium-high heat. Cook tortillas, one at a time, for about 1 minute on each side. Tortillas should be lightly speckled.

✳ NAVAJO FRY BREAD (PAN NAVAJO)

For small servings, the ball of dough should be the size of an egg. For heartier appetites, the dough ball can be the size of a lemon. Fry bread may be served at any breakfast or barbecue.

YIELD: 6–8 servings

INGREDIENTS

2 cups flour

1 tablespoon plus 1 teaspoon
  baking powder

$2/3$ cup warm water

Cornmeal

Shortening or lard

INSTRUCTIONS

Combine flour and baking powder in a large mixing bowl. Add warm water to flour mixture and work into a smooth and elastic dough. Divide dough into balls of desired size. On a board lightly dusted with cornmeal, roll each ball of dough into a circle $1/4$ inch thick. Cut a small hole in the center of each circle.

Heat 2 inches of shortening in a heavy pan at medium-high heat. Fry the dough, one circle at a time, until golden on both sides, turning once. Drain on absorbent towels.

★ BOLILLOS (MEXICAN ROLLS)

I used to make runs to Mexico from San Diego just for these rolls—for the lobster and surfing too, if the truth be told. The little bit of cinnamon adds fragrance and a sweet finish.

YIELD: 24 rolls

INGREDIENTS

$2^2/3$ cup warm water

1 package active dried yeast

1 tablespoon butter, melted

1 heaping tablespoon fructose

1 egg, lightly beaten

5–$6^1/2$ cups unbleached bread flour

$1/2$ cup gluten flour (optional)

$1^1/2$ teaspoons salt

1 teaspoon cinnamon

$1/4$–$1/2$ teaspoon freshly grated
  nutmeg (optional)

$1/2$ teaspoon orange zest

$1/2$ teaspoon lemon zest

(Continued)

INSTRUCTIONS

Mix yeast in $^2/_3$ cup of warm water with butter and fructose. Let stand 5 minutes. Add egg. In a large mixing bowl, combine flour, gluten, salt, cinnamon, nutmeg, orange zest, and lemon zest, and then the remaining water. Mix in yeast mixture until well blended. Turn dough onto a lightly floured surface. Knead for 15 minutes or until dough is smooth and elastic. Place dough in a buttered or sprayed bowl; turn once to moisten top. Cover with plastic wrap and place in a warm, draft-free place for 1 hour or until doubled in bulk.

Punch down dough and turn out onto a lightly floured surface. Form into oblong rolls about 4 inches long, $2^1/_2$ inches wide, and $1^1/_2$–2 inches high. Lightly grease baking sheets with oil and dust with cornmeal. Place rolls on prepared baking sheets. Allow to rise until nearly doubled in size, 30–45 minutes.

Preheat oven to 375°F. With a sharp knife, cut $^1/_2$-inch-deep diagonal slashes the length of each roll; brush with cold water. Bake for 25–35 minutes or until rolls are golden brown and sound hollow when lightly tapped. Remove from baking sheet to a wire rack to cool. Guests can break the bolillos apart at the table and dip them in the Sopa de la Casa or spread with a sweet citrus butter.

MEXICAN BREAD PUDDING (CAPIROTADA)

This dessert is a Lenten specialty in Mexico, classic and tempting. The recipe calls for walnuts, but peanuts, pine nuts, or almonds may be substituted. Try using pears for a sweet finish. More dried fruit can be added than is called for in the recipe. Toss in chopped prunes or any other dried fruit. The most important ingredient, of course, is the bread, which must be absolutely dry yet untoasted and, if possible, homemade. Sweet French bread, bolillo, or pan dulce is best. The interesting addition is the cheese.

YIELD: 24 servings

INGREDIENTS

$1^{1}/_{2}$ pounds brown sugar

2 whole cloves

2 sticks cinnamon, each about 2 inches in length

1 cup evaporated skim milk

$^{1}/_{2}$ pound butter

4 medium apples, both green and red, cored and diced

1 quart boiling water

2 quarts stale French bread cubes, $^{3}/_{4}$ inch each

2 cups chopped walnuts

2 cups sultanas or seedless raisins

1 cup currants, diced dates, prunes, or dried apricots

$^{1}/_{2}$ pound Monterey Jack cheese, grated

$^{1}/_{2}$ pound Longhorn Cheddar cheese, grated

2 teaspoons cinnamon

2 teaspoons vanilla extract

INSTRUCTIONS

Add brown sugar, cloves, cinnamon sticks, milk, and butter to the boiling water and allow to boil uncovered until a light syrup forms (the mixture will become more viscous and should just coat the back of a spoon). Add diced apple during last 5 minutes to soften slightly. Remove cloves and cinnamon sticks.

Preheat oven to 350°F. In a large, buttered baking dish or springform pan, distribute bread cubes, chopped nuts, sultanas, currants, Monterey Jack, and Cheddar. Lift apples from syrup and distribute over bread. Add cinnamon and vanilla to syrup and spoon or pour evenly over the bread and apples. With back of spoon, press bread mixture to soak it with syrup. Bake for 30–35 minutes.

✳ PASSIONFRUIT OR POMEGRANATE SAUCE

This is luscious over baked or grilled bananas or fruit medley, rice and bread pudding, frozen yogurt, or your own imaginative dessert.

YIELD: $3^{1}/_{2}$ cups

(Continued)

INGREDIENTS

$^1/_2$ cup sugar or fructose

$^3/_4$ cup orange juice

9 ounces dried apricots or 18 fresh
apricots

3 passion fruit, pomegranates,
or guava

$^3/_4$ cup water or as needed

Brandy or Grand Marnier to flambé

INSTRUCTIONS

Combine orange juice, sugar, or fructose, and apricots and simmer in small
saucepan. Cut passionfruit in half crosswise; scoop out pulp and seeds. (If using
pomegranate, seed it—and good luck!; if using guava, chop up fruit). Stir pulp
into the apricot mixture and bring back to simmer for an additional 10 minutes,
adding water to thin. Remove from heat and chill. Blend or purée until smooth.
Before serving, add alcohol and flambé sauce.

★ GREEN CHILE SPOONBREAD

*Vary the filling with colorful and flavorful additions such as diced red or yellow pep-
per, chopped cilantro, sliced green onion, and minced jalapeños. This will wake up
customers' palates, especially when served with scrambled eggs and a hot and creamy
sauce. This formula may easily be turned to muffins and could be served with
whipped cream cheese and jalapeño jelly.*

YIELD: 24 servings

INGREDIENTS

2 cups cornmeal

2 cups whole-wheat pastry flour

1 tablespoon plus 1 teaspoon baking
powder

2 teaspoons baking soda

1 tablespoon chili powder

1–2 teaspoons salt

2 pints plain nonfat yogurt

4 cans cream-style or whole kernel
corn, $8^3/_4$ ounces each

4 eggs, beaten

2–4 egg whites, whipped

2 cans diced green chiles, 4 ounces
each

1 pound Monterey Jack cheese, grated

INSTRUCTIONS

Preheat oven to 350°F. Combine cornmeal, pastry flour, baking powder, baking soda, chili powder, and salt. Make a well in center and add yogurt, corn, and eggs. Pour half of mixture into two buttered or sprayed 9 × 9 pans. Top with half of the green chiles and half of the cheese. Repeat layers. Bake for 35–40 minutes.

* BI-BELL MUFFINS

Add a few jalapeños, $^1/_4$ cup diced red bell peppers, and $^1/_4$ cup diced green bell peppers. Heat oiled muffin pan in 375°F oven first and then add batter to hot pan.

* STUFFED BANANA NUT FRENCH TOAST

This gala, rich breakfast entrée has a sweet and creamy surprise inside. Serve with warm maple syrup, a drizzle of honey, or flambéed with Grand Marnier and syrup. My gourmet mother suggests using a grapefruit knife to slice into the center of each bread wedge (See Color Plate 22).

YIELD: 8 servings

INGREDIENTS

2 eggs

2 egg whites

$^2/_3$–$^3/_4$ cup nonfat milk

1 banana

$^1/_2$ teaspoon kosher salt or sea salt

$^1/_4$–$^1/_3$ cup diced walnuts, pecans, or macadamia nuts

1 teaspoon vanilla or Grand Marnier

1 teaspoon cinnamon

1 teaspoon ground ginger

$^1/_2$ teaspoon nutmeg, freshly grated

8 thick-cut slices firm white bread

4 ounces nonfat cream cheese

4 ounces Grand Marnier plum jam (or your choice)

(Continued)

INSTRUCTIONS

Process eggs, egg whites, milk, banana, salt, nuts, vanilla, cinnamon, ginger, and nutmeg in food processor or blender. Pour into a large shallow dish. Spread the inside center of diagonally sliced slices of bread with cream cheese and jam; dip into egg mixture on both sides.

Heat a griddle or large skillet over medium-low heat, then spray with oil. Brown bread slices, about 5 minutes on each side. Serve with fruit butter, quark, marmalade, honey, maple syrup, or jam, or flambé with Grand Marnier.

CEREALS

Healthy cereals, such as granola and muesli, may be made from scratch so that you can monitor the amount of brown sugar, honey, and nuts added. Blending your own also yields up to two thirds savings. The mix may be used in yeast breads and muffins, as a topping, and in layered parfaits.

Blended cereals may be used as edible props in clear canisters from which guests may help themselves. Provide banana chips, dried cranberries, cherries, nuts, and raisins as your budget permits. Introduce a new high-fiber grain, such as Kashi and wheat berries, for a novel taste. Refer to the granola variations list for ingredient ideas. Serve cereal with soy, skim, or rice milk and a fresh fruit topping.

Bagelby's serves twenty-one varieties of bagels baked from scratch throughout the day. Their challenge is offering all the flavors fresh every hour. This is met by thorough tracking and recorded sales, resulting in a finely tuned par to build to. Bagelby's baskets make attractive props on a back wall. The baker tries to keep them two-thirds full, fresh, and aromatic. Onion, garlic, and seeded bagels are kept in the lower baskets to prevent aromas and flavors from intermingling.

Breakfast breads and sandwiches to go are a great hit for local Coeur d'Alene businesses. Bagelby's makes up beautiful trays with cut and whole fruits, assorted bagels, and flavored cream cheese spreads. The most popular bagel varieties are cinnamon raisin and other flavors reminiscent of comfort food. Heartier breakfast sandwiches include the lox and cream cheese classic garnished with sliced tomatoes, red onions, lemons, and capers. Mini-bagels are available for lighter appetites.

Granola is great as a snack, breakfast cereal, and even dessert with ground dried fruits and nuts. Follow the basic recipe below but vary ingredients according to your preference. After mixing, simply bake in a sheet pan or hotel pan at 350°F for 15 minutes, stirring every 5 minutes. Museli, too, is easy. Soak 1 cup rolled oats overnight in 1 cup boiling water, then mix in 2 tablespoons lemon juice and fruits and nuts of choice.

GRANOLA VARIATIONS

Cereals	Fruits	Nuts/Seeds	Flavorings
Buckwheat groats	Apples, grated or dried	Almonds	Allspice
Cornmeal	Apricots, chopped	Cashews, raw or regular	Cinnamon
Corn, wheat, rye flakes	Coconut, shredded	Hazelnuts, filberts	Orange peel
Puffed cereal, rice, spelt, or millet	Dates, chopped	Macadamia nuts	Pumpkin pie spice
Rolled oats	Orange zest	Peanuts	Vanilla
Wheat germ, regular or toasted	Dried cherries, berries	Pumpkin seeds	Oil
Wheat bran	Prunes, pitted, chopped	Pine nuts	Honey
Kashi	Raisins or sultanas	Sunflower seeds	Maple syrup
		Walnuts	Molasses
			Orange flower water

✳ HEALTH GRANOLA WITH DRIED FRUITS AND NUTS

The increased economy, flavor, and nutritional value of making your own granola mix is certain.

YIELD: 12 servings

(Continued)

INGREDIENTS

2 cups old-fashioned oats, uncooked

2 cups buckwheat groats

2 cups wheat flakes

1 cup sesame seeds

1 cup pumpkin seeds

1 cup walnuts

1 cup almonds

2 tablespoons zest of orange

1 teaspoon cinnamon

1 teaspoon nutmeg

2 cups raisins, dried apricots, dried
    cranberries, or dried cherries

1 cup coconut

1 cup honey

$1/2$ cup butter, melted

INSTRUCTIONS

Preheat oven to 350°F. Mix all ingredients thoroughly. Spread mixture on cookie sheet; bake for 20–25 minutes, stirring every 5 minutes.

Oatmeal and cream of wheat and rice are the classic hot cereals to "scoop and serve" off the steam table. Garnish colorfully with diagonal stripes of toasted coconut, raisins, chopped nuts, and diced fruits or berries, or even just canned sliced apples.

BREAKFAST POTATOES

Breakfast potatoes are an easy option and hold up well on the steam table. Creamy O'Brien scalloped potatoes work well, as does Little Joe's Scramble with eggs, cheese, spinach, and onion. Potato pancakes may be made ahead and arrayed attractively on a tray or steam pan. Consult the color chart for garnish ideas—stamped cut-outs, dice, or julienne of colored peppers or long shreds of root vegetables of any color. Dollop sour cream, scatter sliced ripe olives or minced parsley, pipe puréed root vegetable, or drop an edible flower or two over each dish. Remember to place ornamental kale in the corners.

POTATO LATKES

In my variation of this classic Jewish recipe, I use grated Asiago or Parmesan cheese to bind the golden and emerald flecks of crookneck squash, zucchini, and grated potatoes. Latkes reheat easily and can be wrapped in an aluminum foil packet to take on the run. They look colorful layered on a half or full hotel pan with dollops of sour cream. Serve applesauce separately or make sandwiches of two pancakes and kefir or Neufchâtel cheese (see Color Plate 23).

YIELD: 24 pancakes, 3 inches in diameter

INGREDIENTS

4 medium baking potatoes, peeled and grated

2 zucchini, shredded

2 crookneck squash, shredded

$^1/_2$ cup green onion, minced

$^1/_2$ cup Asiago or Parmesan cheese, grated

4 eggs

4–6 tablespoons parsley, minced

1 tablespoon butter

1 tablespoon safflower oil

GARNISHES

Sour cream or kefir

Applesauce

INSTRUCTIONS

Wrap grated potatoes in a clean tea towel or cheesecloth; press to absorb moisture. Stir together potatoes, zucchini, crookneck squash, green onion, cheese, eggs, and parsley.

In a large skillet, heat butter and oil. Drop pancake batter into the oil by heaping spoonfuls and flatten to 3-inch patties about $^1/_4$ inch thick. Fry until crisp and brown on both sides.

Serve very hot with sour cream and applesauce. (To keep latkes warm, place on paper towels on a baking sheet in a 200°F oven.)

Bed and breakfast operations such as the Hayden Hideaway and Susan's Sybaritic Culinary Center on Lake Coeur d'Alene find great success with homemade granolas and brunch potatoes for hungry skiers. Granolas and muesli are displayed prominently in clear canisters tied with a jaunty, bright bow around the neck. Overnight guests scoop out as much as they wish and add local huckleberries, boysenberries, and other fresh fruits. Colorful dried fruits and nuts lend flavor and crunch.

Potato pancakes, squash-laden latkes, and O'Brien potatoes are always winners, especially when garnished with sour cream, applesauce, and other tasty toppings. Southwest chicken chili hash is a hit, too, with eggs and bold wake-up flavors.

An easy dish that's a godsend to fatigued inn owners is Idaho Potato Bacon Pie. Like a strata, it may be made the night before. Cooked potatoes (4 cups) are grated or mashed coarsely to bits and layered with salt, pepper, 1/2 cup milk, and 12 slices of cooked bacon, crumbled. The flavors meld overnight; then the kitchen smells great the next morning when the pie is baked at 375°F for 30 minutes. Ricotta or cottage cheese may be substituted for 1 1/2 cups of the potato for a lighter, fluffier version. While the potato pie bakes, the eggs and fruit shakes are prepared.

BREAKFAST SOUPS AND SHAKES

Fruit soups and shakes are breakfast ideas that don't require a recipe. Purée any melon with 1 cup mixed fruits. Flute the melon shells for attractive serving containers. Flavor fruit purée with almond or vanilla extract, Kirsch, orange or lemon peel, or candied ginger. Thicken with plain yogurt, quark, ice milk, or frozen yogurt. Thin with fruit juice. For a nutritious finish, add a bit of brewers' yeast, kelp, high-protein powder, wheat germ, seeds, nuts, or nonfat dry milk powder.

Serve in attractive tall glassware in a variety of shapes. Build up an eclectic mix of glassware, props, and even plastic glasses from company samples, outlets, garage sales, and other nonrestaurant avenues. For your own juice bar set-up, review the shake chart on page 160 for a list of starting ingredients (see Color Plate 24.)

Fast Fruit Shakes

★ SUPERSTARTER

This is like refreshing, creamy rocket fuel at the start of the day. Infinite in variations, tasty in flavor, and many-hued, depending on the fruits and berries used, it is suitable for both brunches and to-go.

YIELD: 1 serving

INGREDIENTS

$^1/_2$ cup peaches, sliced

$^1/_4$ cup orange, cranberry, or apple juice

$^1/_4$ cup plain nonfat yogurt

1 teaspoon brown sugar or honey

$^1/_4$ teaspoon lemon juice

$^1/_4$ teaspoon cinnamon

3 ice cubes

GARNISH

Mint sprig

INSTRUCTIONS

Blend or process ingredients until smooth. Garnish with sprig of fresh mint.

Substitute $^1/_2$ cup diced cantaloupe or $^1/_2$ cup drained mandarin orange segments for peaches.

✳ BANANA FRAPPE

Add as many extra ingredients as your guest desires, for an additional price.

YIELD: 8 servings

INGREDIENTS

4 bananas, peeled and sliced

$1/_4$ cup orange juice

$1/_4$ cup grapefruit juice

$1/_4$ cup apple juice

$1/_4$ cup plain nonfat yogurt

1 tablespoon plus 1 teaspoon wheat germ

1 tablespoon lecithin powder

2 teaspoons kelp

2 teaspoons blue-green algae

2 teaspoons brewer's yeast

20 ice cubes

GARNISHES

Grapefruit wheels, halved

Orange slices

Lemon wheels

Mint sprigs

INSTRUCTIONS

In blender, blend all ingredients in batches for 1 minute on high until smooth and creamy. Pour into frosted, stemmed goblets and garnish with citrus wheels and sprigs of mint.

KID- AND ADULT-FRIENDLY FRUIT SMOOTHIE

YIELD: 1 serving

INGREDIENTS

4 ounces fruit(s) of choice, thawed
   if frozen

3 ounces orange juice, fresh or frozen

1 ounce lemon juice, fresh squeezed

8 ounces crushed ice

4 ounces nonfat vanilla frozen yogurt

1 tablespoon honey

GARNISHES

Fresh fruit slices

Kiwi wheel

Whole strawberry

Mint sprig

INSTRUCTIONS

Place all ingredients in blender; process until mixture is frosty and smooth. Pour into a 16-ounce cup or tall glass and serve with garnish.

PURPLE COWS

Use 5 ounces of blackberry puree or frozen blackberries, $\frac{1}{2}$ cup evaporated skim milk (or whole milk or half & half) a four ounce scoop of nonfat vanilla frozen yogurt, 8 ounces of crushed ice and 1–2 tablespoons honey. Garnish with a mint sprig and one berry on top.

BLUE BANANA BLOOPER

Use 4 ounces frozen blueberries, 4 ounces of sliced frozen (or fresh bananas), 2 ounces cranraspberry or purple grape juice, 1 ounce lemon juice, 8 ounces crushed ice, 1 tablespoon honey. Garnish with a lemon wheel and sprig of mint placed at a sprightly angle.

✳ *FAST FRUIT SHAKE*

Use 4 ounces sliced frozen or fresh nectarines or peaches, $^1/_4$ cup apple, orange or passionfruit juice, $^1/_4$–$^1/_2$ teaspoon cinnamon, 1 ounce plain nonfat yogurt, 1 tablespoon lemon juice, 8 ounces crushed ice, 1 tablespoon honey. Garnish with a fruit slice of peaches, lime wheel (or lemon), and sprig of mint at a jaunty angle.

✳ *PAPAYA SPLASH*

Use 4 ounces papaya or mango slices, $^1/_2$ cup lemonade, frozen and reconstituted or orange juice (fresh or frozen), 1 tablespoon honey, 8 ounces crushed ice, $^1/_4$–$^1/_2$ teaspoon freshly grated ginger root. Garnish with wedge of papaya, mango, orange wheels, and/or fresh peppermint sprigs.

✳ *MAGIC SUPER STARTER*

Use 4 ounces peaches, 2 ounces raspberries or blackberries, 2 ounces sliced bananas, $^1/_2$ cup cranraspberry or blueberry juice, 2 to 3 ice cubes, 1 tablespoon lemon, 1 tablespoon honey, $^1/_4$–$^1/_2$ teaspoon cinnamon, and freshly grated nutmeg. Garnish with lemon or lime wheel and mint sprig.

✳ *FRUIT NOG*

Use 6 ounces fruit of your choice, 2 tablespoons frozen orange juice concentrate, $^1/_4$ cup skim milk, 1 tablespoon honey, $^1/_4$ teaspoon vanilla, 1 egg, 2 to 3 ice cubes.

✳ *TROPICAL LEMONADE SLUSH*

Use 4 ounces reconstituted lemonade, 4 ounces of sliced mango, papaya, peaches, or halved apricots, 2 ounces sliced bananas, 8 ounces crushed ice, 1 tablespoon lemon juice, and 1 tablespoon honey. Replace banana with any berry for a pink finish. Garnish with lemon wheel and mint sprig.

✳ *HUNZA LONGEVITY CHOCOLATE DRINK*

Use 2 ounces sliced bananas, 4 ounces chocolate syrup (nonfat), 6 ounces vanilla frozen yogurt, 6 ounces crushed ice, 1 ounce peanut butter, 1 tablespoon malt or high protein powder. Garnish with whipped cream, chocolate curls, and a real cherry on top.

✳ *ORANGE BANANA CREAM*

Use $^1/_2$ cup orange juice, $^1/_2$ cup vanilla ice cream or evaporated skim milk, 1 tablespoon creamy or chunky peanut butter, $^1/_2$ small ripe banana, quartered, orange marmalade to taste for a sweeter shake, and three ice cubes. Garnish with a candied orange wheel and mint sprig with whipped cream, if desired.

✳ REVITALIZER

This was a favorite drink at Cal-a-Vie, a California spa where I cooked and taught nutrition seminars and cooking classes.

YIELD: 16 servings

INGREDIENTS

48 ounces canned vegetable cocktail juice

72 ounces water ($1^1/_2$ vegetable juice cans)

2 celery stalks, chopped coarse

1 large carrot, chopped coarse

1 bunch parsley

1 bay leaf

2 teaspoons red pepper flakes

2 teaspoons whole rosemary

$^1/_2$ teaspoon fennel seed

4 fresh basil sprigs

2 cups mixed vegetables (mushrooms, tomatoes, onions, red pepper, green pepper, snow peas)

INSTRUCTIONS

Put all ingredients into a 2-quart stockpot. Simmer over low heat for 40 minutes. Strain broth into a pitcher and discard the vegetables. Serve hot or cold.

Ingredients for Fast Shakes

Select one ingredient from each category in the amount specified, or use two ingredients from the same category (such as peaches and pineapple), each in half the amount specified for that category. Make a fruitier or creamier shake by omitting a category and increasing the proportions for the ingredients you prefer.

Fruits (1/2 cup)	Dairy Products (1/4 cup)	Juice (1/4 cup)	Flavorings (1/4–1/2 teaspoon)	Nutritious Additions
Apples	Buttermilk	Apple	Almond extract	Brewer's yeast
Apricots	Cottage cheese	Carrot	Brown sugar	Carob powder
Bananas	Cream cheese	Coconut	Cinnamon	High-protein powder
Berries	Egg, whole	Cranberry	Ginger	Nonfat dry milk
Dates	Ice cream, ice milk, or frozen yogurt	Grapefruit	Grape jelly	Lecithin powder
Kiwi fruit	Milk, skim, whole, or nonfat dry	Orange	Honey	Peanut butter
Mandarin oranges	Whipping cream	Papaya	Instant coffee	Sesame seeds
Lemons	Yogurt, plain or flavored	Pineapple	Lemon juice	Sunflower seeds
Melons		Peach	Mint	Wheat germ
Mangoes		Strawberry	Nutmeg	
Limes			Orange marmalade	
Papayas			Vanilla	
Peaches				
Pineapples				

Juice bars are coming back in vogue again. The first Good Earth in Palo Alto, California, had a beautiful ice bed of fruits and vegetables in the front window with the juice attendant blending up a storm of frappes, flips, and fizzes. The display of color and rocket-fuel drinks brought in many students from Stanford as well as local residents.

Today at Jungle Juice in Idaho, smoothies of all types are served to the local population. An array of fruits and vegetables features everything from tumbling oranges in the loader bins to cleaned carrots on ice in a Cambro. Wheatgrass is displayed growing in a corner and all is clean and streamlined by friendly, helpful staff.

Eric Wintch and his brother, Shane, have a mission to share the health of juices and smoothies, fruits and vegetables. They present not only a nutritional analysis of each drink but also what each ingredient does for your health. Ginseng, soy protein powder, blue-green algae, echinacea, and ma huang are among the specialty additions available at their store.

BREAKFAST SANDWICHES

Even a sandwich is adaptable for breakfast. Who says a BLT isn't a great option? Especially if you drop the *L* and add cheese or California avocado, mushrooms, onion, red pepper, or sliced olives. Broiled briefly, it becomes a breakfast sandwich. Quesadillas are a Mexican variation that can be half wrapped in colorful squares of foil and shingled on a platter. Other fillings, such as scrambled eggs, salsa, cheese, and meat, hold up well and add variety and interest. Quesadillas and breakfast burritos can also be layered like a torta and cut into wedges right before service.

✴ BROILED BRILLIANT VEGETARIAN SANDWICH

Sauté 1 cup sliced mushrooms, $1/4$ cup diced green or red pepper, $1/4$ cup onion, and $1/4$ cup crookneck squash just until softened. Distribute over 4 slices whole-grain or rye toast. Top each with 1 slice white cheese and a sliced ripe olive. Broil until cheese melts.

✴ AMERICANA FAVORITE

Toast 8 slices raisin bread. Spread 4 with $1/2$ cup peanut butter and the other 4 with 2 mashed bananas or $1/2$ cup spiced apple butter or any other fruit spread. Distribute $1/4$ cup raisins, $1/4$ cup shredded coconut, and $1/4$ cup sliced almonds over peanut butter. Top with toast spread with banana. Quarter for easy eating.

✱ TROPICANA HAM

Top buttered raisin-nut toast with 1 slice baked ham drizzled with a reduction of Hawaiian Punch glaze, 1 slice Swiss cheese, and 1 pineapple ring. Sprinkle with orange zest, cinnamon, and nutmeg. Serve as is or broil to melt cheese.

✱ CROISSANT SANDWICHES

Sprinkle 4 croissants or bialys with a few drops of water and heat in a 350°F oven. Fill with one of the following:

   omelette seasoned with herb of your choice

   slices of Parma or honey-glazed ham, cheese, and pineapple

   cream cheese and a slice of smoked salmon (lox)

Chalupas, Sopes, Gordas, and Garnachas

✱ TORTILLA BOATS

YIELD: 12 tortillas

Chalupa means "small canoe." This edible container is made boat-shaped by pinching dough up around the edges. Start by rolling a $1^1/_2$-inch-diameter ball of tortilla dough into a narrow cylinder about 5 inches long and $^1/_2$ inch wide. Put slantwise into a tortilla press; flatten to about $^1/_4$ inch thick. (For a sopa, make the tortilla dough round, $^1/_4$ inch thick, and $3^1/_2$ inches across.) Bake on a medium-hot comal or frying pan on both sides to partially set the masa. Press center down to cook dough a little more. If the dough appears too thick and doughy in the center, then remove a layer of the dough. Repeat with remaining dough.

   Pinch edges up about $^5/_8$ inch to form a container. Fry, if desired, one at a time in $^1/_4$ inch hot oil or lard (400°F) until golden brown and floating freely, or spoon a little sizzling oil into the center of the sopa, on the dry comal, to cook it. Drain on paper towels.

✳ GORDAS AND MEMELOS

Gordas are little fat tortillas with a little cream or mashed potatoes added to the masa. When a gorda is shaped into a flat football, it becomes a memelo.

✳ GARNACHAS

These large filled tartlets from the Yucatan are authentic and impressive. Usually they are filled with black bean paste (or refried beans), ground beef or picadillo, tomato sauce, and crumbled while cheese. Garnachas make an excellent appetizer or first course.

YIELD: 12 balls

INGREDIENTS

2 cups masa harina

$1^{1}/_{4}$ cups cold water

$^{1}/_{4}$ teaspoon salt

2 cups vegetable oil

INSTRUCTIONS

Mix masa harina, water, and salt together to form a soft dough. Roll the dough into 12 balls, each roughly $1^{3}/_{4}$ inch in diameter. Press each ball of dough onto a floured surface and make a well in it with both thumbs together. Press out the sides of the well and mold dough into a small basket shape about 3 inches across and $^{3}/_{4}$ inch deep. The dough should be about $^{1}/_{4}$ inch thick.

Heat oil in a deep fat fryer until it smokes and fry garnachas, hollow side down first, until pale gold and just a little crisp on the outside. Fry until they float. Drain on absorbent paper and keep warm. Serve as soon as possible, or they become leathery.

HOT LINE/
STEAM TABLE ART

Traditionally, steam table hot lines have been a good way to serve a large volume of food. Unfortunately, some were mediocre in eye and taste appeal, addressing quantity over quality. Heat and hold lines have taken a turn for the better with an emphasis on creativity, theme dining, ethnic and regional foods, and advanced equipment. Hospitals and other food service segments are having great success with theme menus, too.

Pacific Rim cuisine, Southern collard greens, Hawaiian specialties, Italian fare featuring osso bucco, and simple meat and potatoes are colorfully displayed. A certain region of China, such as Szechwan or Canton, may be showcased, with corresponding regional dishes served. Wok cooking may be exhibited on a mobile service cart. Statues, lacquered boxes, and chopsticks may be arranged around the demonstration or serving area (see Color Plate 25). Bally's Hotel in Las Vegas has a beautiful wok arena at their informal buffet.

When planning a menu, be aware of menu cycles and the long-range view. Menu cycles should run from seven days to two weeks, with lots of seasonal cooking. Barbecue, Porterhouse or all-you-can-eat T-bone steaks, seafood,

Italian Day occurs every Tuesday at the Garden Room in Wenatchee, Washington, complete with an Italian flag, banners, posters, and arias in the background. The Italian Institute for Foreign Trade provides materials, props, and promotions to highlight their products without a charge. The staff dress in Italian colors or costumes, wave serving spoons in the air, and cry out "Mangiate!"

Mexican, and Southern food nights are often featured during the week. Holidays allow for a special creative display of props, music, costumes, and garnishes. Labor-intensive dishes such as chiles rellenos may be served only on a regular Thursday Mexican night to attract enough volume to justify the effort. Local purveyors may do the production on these items for a reasonable price.

The trend is to feature exhibition stations—pasta bars with four or five sauces and styles of pasta, shogun grills, cooks and customers creating omelets with individually chosen fillings and toppings. New, too, are rotisseries, carving stations, and wood-fired ovens for roasted vegetables, meats, and pizzas. Dessert stations where Apples Flambé and Flaming Bananas Foster are prepared are great new features. Whatever the meal, dessert is the ever-popular grand finale course. This inherent appeal augments the flair and excitement of individual service, freshness, and the expertise of showtime cooks.

Restaurant mood setting and decor are important as well. The entire ambience now feels more modern, softer, and more commodious. Attention to the small details is bringing about change for the better. Good foods, attractively arranged with a few simple garnishes can elevate the aesthetic encounter. All these touches add up to a more spacious and refined feel to the entire dining experience.

Certainly the heat-and-hold challenges remain the same for steam table lines. Hungry crowds may come all at once for a banquet or after a show as well as during peak meal periods. Setting pars on food inventory and preparation is key. Having backups for everything without wasting food is both important and difficult. This is especially true when banquet numbers quickly change or everyone loves your collard greens so much they take extra helpings. Long-range tracking of customer profiles and preferences through sales tickets aids in setting these par sheets.

Sixth, third, and shallow alley pans may be used for faster turnover. Because there are no waiters, there is no wait, and the staff can monitor and resupply hotel pans and chafing dishes. Often, a single associate is needed to wipe counters and marble borders (basically, to clean up after the customers).

There is little to no cross-panning in the larger hotels and casinos because there is continuous volume and an employee dining room in which to transfer foods. Often these hotels have the opportunity to borrow international dishes from their satellite kitchens with Italian or Chinese specialties. Smaller chains take a pan off the line when it is two-thirds empty. In the kitchen, the third that remains is set atop the new pan and garnished anew. This adds a fresh and flawless presentation to the dish, especially when it is embellished with a unique garnish.

Two styles of hot lines are prevalent in the industry. Dish-up and self-service bars have their own set of challenges but both also can be exhibited well with beautiful presentations, arrangements, props, and garnishes. On the dish-up lines, servers can better control the portioning. The overall look of the scramble or scatter bars is more pleasing and the grazing process gives a feeling of freedom.

Serving bars in the newer buffet lines boast borders of flecked Corian or real marble. Stainless steel does not prevail. The newer look is the scatter or scramble bar approach rather than a long, continuous line. This is more evident in the commercial segments than in the military lines, which must be rigid and straight in minimal amounts of room, especially in submarines. Traffic flows faster with mirror buffets on opposite sides of the room. Self-service is the trend—except at carving stations, where it's best to have the most technically correct cook available slice meats just one dime thick. Self-service on a carving station is not cost-effective. Also, the customers could injure themselves or hack the meat up and leave bones for the others.

Each scatter bar has its own food category with corresponding condiments, garnishes, and propping. Soup and salad bars are most often arranged near the entry, where bright colors can create a good first impression. Kale makes a good border and garnish as it is lacy, colorful—especially purple kale—and lasts three days. Baskets, dried or silk flowers and vegetables on cough guard shelves add to the decor and visual cues. Arrangements of the salad crocks next to a contrasting color introduces a vivid rainbow of choices.

Potato stuffer bars and Mexican taco bars are popular with vegetarian and meat lovers alike. Making each bar festive with a few special strokes of creativity raises the enjoyment level. Simply tying a bright napkin around the soup kettle or to the handle in a jaunty bow brightens the overall presentation. Tucking silk

Another food presentation utilizes the shelf above the entrée hot line for a complete plate visual. Virginia Mason Hospital in Seattle, Washington, displays three or four plated individual servings. This helps the guest to visualize what to order and how to put it all together. The items on the line are designed and matched for compatible flavors and visual appeal. The plate presentations have a special garnish even if the hotel pans do not. The plates themselves are pretty, with a bright rim of color framing the foods.

For serious buffet action, take a food tour of the casinos of Las Vegas. The newest equipment, props, lighting and decor abound here. Chefs are constantly creating new menus and products in consultation with high-profile corporate chefs such as Jim Harvey and Van Atkins of Nestle Food Products, who are always ready to help buffet and steam table operators succeed.

The Nestle chefs and other purveyors of high-quality foods have many tasty and consistent products that work well on a hot line as regional and international specialties. Both steam table—sturdy and easily arranged for eye appeal, such products have a place on hot lines. They can often be brought up to house-special status with a few added ingredients, toppings, and garnishes.

Besides knowing their own product lines thoroughly, these helpful chefs share contacts with equipment and prop specialists. Chef Chet Teel from Main Street Station in downtown Las Vegas was impressed with Van Atkin's culinary skills and speed. Atkins helped design and set up Main Street Station's newly remodeled buffet lines.

Tour as many hotel and casino buffets as possible when in Las Vegas. The chefs are justifiably proud to show you their lines, arrangements, props, pans, and garnishes. Most will bring you to the back to show the pars, panning systems, and color charts and photographs of hotel pan presentations. If you're enamored with a chafing dish or garnish, they may well give you the representative's name or a quick lesson in melon flowers. This is where garde manger excels, with entire departments given over to just cold food work and embellishments.

flowers into a kale border lining an icebar or chilled salad crock bar offers color and liveliness without any "wilt factor."

If the food is colorful and beautifully arranged, time-consuming garnishes may be superfluous. Alternatively, quickly scattered fresh herbs, edible flowers, or julienned tricolored bell peppers, where appropriate, lend a festive and fun touch, rather like confetti. See Chapter 2 for many garnishing ideas.

High-quality equipment and props should always frame appealing, tasty foods. Hot lines are now designed by many stainless steel companies to set the pans at an angle toward the guests. Bright hot lights spotlight the food with warmth and radiance. Adapter sets contain cavities for alley pans, half hotel pans, third pans, and even keyhole inserts for interesting framing. Small round containers are inserted into the adapter frame for sauces and dips. Oval inserts are another choice; tapered fry pans and round and rectangular inserts designed and balanced together provide other options. An angled hotel pan raised up from the steam table line results in an "in-your-face" food presentation. All the new equipment and designs perform well in the presentation, arrangement, and overall quality of buffet lines and trays. Beautiful props and equipment are designed by Giacomo of Regency Service Carts and Bon Chef.

Cough guards have evolved into a clear canopy with an added shelf that provides a base for flowers, ivy, bottles, or baskets as well as a covering for the foods. New serving pieces—iron skillets, paella pans, brass-handled oval dishes, and copper pans of all varieties—generate more interest than the typical rectangular hotel pans.

Deli cases are available now in the European style, with curved glass and staggered shelving for enticing views. Shelving can be ordered in jet black or granite Corian. Grape leaves, cut-outs, streamers, flowers, and produce, whole or cut, as well as holiday props, are just some of what can embellish the display beyond the food. Props, containers, and crocks are available in any number of colors, shapes, and sizes.

If you've inherited older or utilitarian props, these too can be brightened with a little ingenuity. Visit a local fabric store and look for remnants that may be tied around the containers and knotted. Pinking shears prevent most unraveling of threads, which obviates the need to sew hems around each edge. Watching garage sales and sell-outs in import stores can reward you with a bundle of multicolored napkins. These may be tied around crocks or laid underneath containers.

Old iron pots, heated first, may be poised above candles. Iron pots, kettles, and Griswold's skillets retain heat for quite a while on their own, too. This would be authentic for off-premise catering, especially if you're doing an outdoor covered wagon round-up. Nothing needs to match; eclectic is in. Check out stores selling used restaurant supplies and big hotels replacing and eliminating lines of copper or even silver chafers. You may find quite a deal.

Whatever the equipment and props may be, your food can be presented with enticing appeal. All of the elements of art can be embodied right in the hotel pan. By arranging the food nicely in the pan with a simple contrasting garnish, you're on the way to edible art.

HOT LINE OVERVIEW

In planning your buffet, think of the line or each bar as canvas to be painted with colors. Design your pans or platters and hot line layout, props, and fabrics based on the menu. Relate the colors to the overall buffet and each pan or tray in itself. Separate colors; use a color wheel to show the primary colors and their opposites. Contrast is the key.

Put texture in every pan and on each tray. Crunch may be had by a topping of nuts, a sprinkling of tortilla chips, or other crunchy garnishes. This adds body and gives good mouth-feel.

The shapes of foods should take different forms. This creates appetizing con-

Characteristic	Spectrum	Example
Aroma	Faint/strong	Vanilla custard with cinnamon
Color	Varied	Tropical fruit salad
Consistency	Fatty/astringent	Salmon with horseradish
Cooked state	Cooked/raw	Zabaglione with strawberries
Cost	Inexpensive/expensive	Potatoes and caviar
Density	Heavy/light	Lemon meringue pie
Familiarity	Common/exotic	Mashed potatoes and huitlacoche
Flavor	Sweet/sour/salty/bitter	Pad Thai
Flavor strength	Sharp/bland	Lemon sole
Moistness	Wet/dry	Soup with croutons
Size	Big/little	Steak with fingerling potatoes
Spiciness/hotness	Spicy-hot/bland-cool	Wasabi on tuna sushi
Temperature	Hot/cold	Hot apple pie with cream
Texture	Crispy/soft	Grilled cheese sandwich

trast and interest. Take naturally shaped foods and contrast them with molded foods. A rice timbale centered in a chafing dish with fish fillets swimming in a moat of lemon butter sauce à la meunière is an admirable example. Red and green grapes, like rubies and emeralds, may be scattered over each piece of fish. The lemon-lime rice enhances the sauce and may have flecks of parsley with the citrus zest (see Color Plate 26).

Finally, flavors and aromas are the elements beyond art that we have to draw upon. Above is a great chart for menu planning based on contrasting flavors, culled from *Culinary Artistry*.*

Contrasts Among Ingredients

Providing contrasts within a dish offers powerful opportunities for heightened interest as well as expressing one's point of view. Most important, it is a way to achieve the all-important sense of balance in a dish.

FISH AND SEAFOOD

New species of seafood are available these days, despite the extinction of some precious varieties. Source the nontraditional species for cost savings as well as op-

*By Andrew Donenburg and Karen Page (published by John Wiley & Sons, Inc. © 1996).

portunity for your customers to try something new. New Zealand blue cod is a delicious fish similar to sea bass but priced more like pollock. Adhere to all purchasing principles when choosing and receiving the fish. Specifications, standards, backup purveyors, and handling the fish reverentially are key to presenting flawless fish.

When cooking fish, employ the 10-minutes-per-inch rule: Cook the fish for 10 minutes per inch of thickness of the fillet, regardless of method. Cooking methods include baking, broiling, grilling, pan frying, and poaching but not microwaving.

When sautéing fish, begin with clarified butter or spray in a nonstick pan on medium-high heat. Place filets nice side down first (skin side up) for best appearance, without overcrowding. This achieves even coloring and cooking.

When the edges of the fish start to curl and turn opaque, flip the fillets over. This should take $1\frac{1}{2}$–2 minutes for a thin sole fillet. (Thicker fillets and steaks of swordfish and tuna hold up best on the steam table.)

The next indicator, within 2 minutes, is for the overall fillet to turn from translucent to opaque. It should flake slightly. If there is a golden crust, use the tines of a fork to prod gently. Check the thickest portion to see if it flakes; try not to mar the fillet. When the fish is opaque and flakes easily, remove it to a chafer or serving dish. Serve in purist fashion with lemon wedges and a sprinkling of parsley, or with a simple sauce. Refer to recipes and variations.

Scallops, shrimp, lobster, and crab cook similarly; their flesh turns from translucent to opaque or solid in color while remaining somewhat moist.

Live mussels, clams, and oysters pop open when cooked. Don't try to pry closed ones open to eat them. Shucked oysters firm slightly and their edges curl when cooked.

Fish sticks too, follow the 10-minutes-an-inch rule. Fry them until they float or, better yet, bake them until golden brown. These can be more appetizing by arranging them in patterns across a bed of black bean and roasted corn relish. Add dollops of Jalapeño Honey Tartar Sauce for extra flavor and an element of surprise—it looks like regular tartar sauce but has small green flecks of minced jalapeño. Flute a bell pepper cup and fill with more tartar sauce for those that like it *hot*. Place in a corner of the hotel pan or alongside for self-service.

Present seafood with surrounding props such as brightly colored papier-mâché fish on the cough guard shelf. Display a seafood magazine or cookbook. Hand out a recipe for an easy home-cooked fish dish, explaining the 10-minutes-per-inch rule. Perhaps acquire a hanging mobile of fish to swim in the air above the seafood chafer. Use a full-gloved salmon-shaped pot holder to serve the fish. Wear a yellow slicker and bright yellow matching Sou'wester hat while dishing up fish. Then you can tell the guests you caught it all yourself and make them smile before dining.

The classic garnishes are fluted lemons and limes. Why not add a fluted orange? Skewer all three and pierce a cornered fish at a rakish angle in the hotel pan. Scatter very thinly sliced lemon and lime wheels over fish. Sprigs of dill are appropriate if part of the sauce. This also lets guests know quickly whether or not they'd love the dish.

Serve a fish dish with tropical flavors—fruit chutney or colorful fruit salsa—for a change. Whole or large cuts of the relish ingredients could serve as garnishes in the corner of a pan. Place the top of a pineapple and skewered baby bananas in the corner of a chafing dish. Sautéed bananas in golden Parmesan cheese are great with any fish fillet. A coronet of kiwi next to a halved papaya with contrasting mint sprigs adds color, verve, and interest to the presentation. Papaya and kiwi relish with toasted coconut and mint also may be strewn over fish or placed alongside for self-service. Use a small serving spoon for product extension and lowered food cost.

The arrangement in the pan may be pleasingly attractive in itself. Sometimes there is no need for a garnish at all; the recipe or dish may have so many colorful elements that adding another shape or color for final garnish may be superfluous. Present any type or recipe of fish with rice pilaf mounded along the sides of the pan for a change from the timbale mold in the middle.

Serve a Cajun-style Salmon-Stuffed Trout on a bed of dirty rice. Placing grilled salmon steaks on stoneground grits or pillows of polenta raises the fish from the bottom of the pan and makes a contrasting support that frames the individual serving. Thicker cuts and fish on the bone fall apart less readily in the pan. Try this distinctive presentation: place Seafood Newburg or another mixture in scallop shells on rock salt right in the pan (see Color Plate 27). Fish en papillote make nice little packages to set on the rock salt or on colored rices (see Color Plate 28); the fish and garnish can show right through the paper. Puff pastry shells make rich, edible containers for crab fondue mixture, Coquilles Saint-Jacques, and Fruits de Mer Mornay.

Sauced seafood such as Seafood au Gratin or Creamy Peppercorn Béchamel may create its own garnish as it bakes. Baked noodle or seafood casseroles with cheese may take an extra garnish of cubed cheeses. Arrange different colored cubes in a design on the top of the casserole. As the dish bakes, the cheeses melt and blend together to form a colorful top layer. Surrounding the dish with toasted breadcrumbs or crushed tortilla chips enhances the final presentation.

Other Southwestern treatments of seafood include a sizzling seafood fajita mix served with traditional accompaniments and fish verde with a lime, cilantro, avocado, and tomatillo sauce enriched with cream cheese and dusted with chopped toasted almonds. Swordfish Manzanita holds up well broiled, grilled, or baked with salsa. Garnish abundantly with diced chiles, red onion, and green bell peppers, chopped parsley mixed with cilantro, sliced green onions, and dollops of sour cream topped with a California ripe olive. Seafood Veracruz features a classic sauce that freezes well and doubles as a pasta or potato sauce. The pleasing bite of jalapeños is a nice counterpoint to the sweetness of cinnamon, cloves, and refreshing zest of lemon and cilantro.

Seafood Selection Guide

Use this chart to identify species of fish that share characteristics of flavor and texture. If the fish you planned to purchase is not available, find a good substitute here. Take advantage of the best buys while becoming familiar with the wide variety of fish available in today's market.

	Flavor	
Mild	Moderate	Full
Delicate Texture		
Flounder, sole	Catfish	Herring, Sardine
Orange roughy	Whiting, hake	Smelt
Skate	Pink salmon	Eel
Sea trout, weakfish		Butterfish
Alaska pollock		
Medium-Firm Texture		
Cod	Ocean perch	Atlantic salmon
Haddock	Striped bass	King salmon
Halibut	Chum salmon	Mackerel
Tilefish	Porgy, scup	Amberjack
Grouper	Drums	Sockeye salmon
Snapper	Buffalofish	Sablefish
Tilapia	Rainbow trout	Bluefish
Cusk	Mahimahi	Carp
Ocean pout	Black sea bass	Pomfret
Wolffish	Atlantic pollock	Yellowtail
Skate	Pompano	
Bream	Perch	
Firm Texture		
Monkfish	Shark	Chilean sea bass
Kingklip	New Zealand blue cod	Tuna
	Sturgeon	Swordfish

Seafood lines are a challenge to heat and hold if the fish is delicate. It is better for all food service segments to use hearty, firm fish.

✱ Marinated Shark Steaks

I developed this recipe for many a catered affair. The marinade is great for poultry as well. The creamy mustard plaster adds a rich finish to the fish. It is easy to increase this formula to any number you may need. Any fillet of fish may be substituted as well.

YIELD: 4 servings

INGREDIENTS

4 shark (or swordfish) steaks,
   6–8 ounces each

2 teaspoons safflower or any light oil

2 tablespoons light soy sauce
   or tamari

1 tablespoon fresh lemon or lime juice

1/2 cup dry white wine

1 teaspoon chopped fresh tarragon

3 tablespoons minced scallions, white
   parts only

2 tablespoons Pommery or
   Dijon-style mustard

2 tablespoons evaporated skim milk,
   nonfat cream cheese, or Quark

INSTRUCTIONS

Place steaks in shallow baking dish. Combine oil, soy sauce, lemon juice, wine, tarragon, and scallions in a bowl, and pour over the fish. Turn steaks to coat the other side, cover, and refrigerate for 2 hours. Combine mustard and milk, and set aside.

   Preheat the broiler or barbecue. Broil or grill steaks 3 to 4 inches from the heat for about 12 minutes (10 minutes an inch of thickness) or until fish browns lightly and is moist but opaque. During the last few minutes, divide the mustard mixture among the steaks, spreading a little on each. Serve with lemon wedges or slices and a sprightly sprig of parsley.

CREAMY PEPPERCORN SCALLOPS

Use the smaller quantities for lunch servings, the larger for dinner.

YIELD: 2 servings (sauce recipe yields 44 ounces)

INGREDIENTS

PEPPERCORN SAUCE

$2^1/_2$ cups heavy cream

1 pint Chablis

4 ounces Knorr Swiss white sauce mix

2 ounces Green peppercorns, drained

2 ounces Dijon or Pommery mustard

2 ounces Sour cream (fat free or regular)

SCALLOPS

8–10 ounces sea scallops or any seafood mix

$^1/_2$ ounce butter

INSTRUCTIONS

For the sauce, mix Chablis and cream. Stir in white sauce mix with wire whip. Heat in a small stockpot or 3-quart saucepan on low heat to 180°F. Add peppercorns, mustard, and sour cream. Remove from heat. Sauce should be *thick*.

Sauté scallops (do not pat dry before sautéing) in butter. Add sauce and heat thoroughly.

Serve with 2 ounces of sauce in a small scallop shell or oval casserole for a lunch dish. Use a large scallop shell or oval casserole for a dinner dish and serve with 3 ounces of sauce.

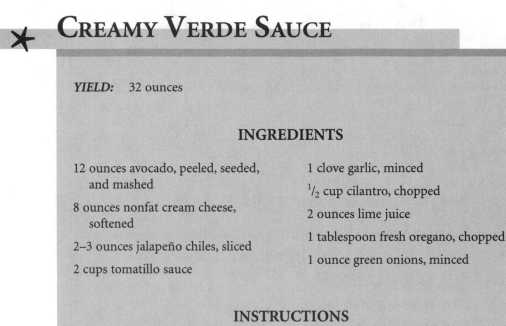

✴ CREAMY VERDE SAUCE

YIELD: 32 ounces

INGREDIENTS

12 ounces avocado, peeled, seeded,
   and mashed

8 ounces nonfat cream cheese,
   softened

2–3 ounces jalapeño chiles, sliced

2 cups tomatillo sauce

1 clove garlic, minced

$^1/_2$ cup cilantro, chopped

2 ounces lime juice

1 tablespoon fresh oregano, chopped

1 ounce green onions, minced

INSTRUCTIONS

Blend all ingredients; place in covered, dated container and refrigerate.

POULTRY AND HEARTIER MEATS

"Poultry" wrote Brillat-Savarin in 1825, "is for the cook what a canvas is to the painter. Its mild flavor, adaptability and almost universal availability have made it central to the cuisines of the world." The versatility of poultry is evident wherever it is eaten—which is almost everywhere.

Dining today emphasizes balance, variety, and aesthetic presentation. Poultry fits into this sensible, artistic style of eating. Cariana Cristiano of Nino's in Long Beach, California, says, "Chicken and poultry is the entrée of the decade as seafood was in the eighties and veal in the seventies." (See Color Plate 29.)

Food service supervisors are buying more poultry because it offers convenience, value, and nutrition as well as good taste. Both chicken and turkey are excellent, economical sources of high-quality protein; they are also low in fat and calories and available in a variety of forms—whole, cut up, ground, formed into roasts, smoked, and processed into cold cuts.

Of course, the least expensive poultry is the least processed. However, the best in value may not be the poultry with the lowest price per pound; also to be taken into account is the yield or number of servings per pound. Chicken and other poultry may be roasted, baked, grilled, broiled, sautéed, deep-fried, stir-fried, stewed, braised, poached, or made into stocks, soup, and sauces.

For hot line purposes, all poultry cuts are great. Only the boneless chicken breasts need extra care; serve them sauced or at least quickly so they don't dry out. Turkey tenderloins are a delicious change. Pounded, they almost taste like veal, but they have enough flavor to stand up to intense sauces. The sauces also prevent the cutlets from drying out. Treated like veal, turkey offers an excellent substitute at an affordable price. Simply call your entrée dish cutlets Picatta, Marsala, Saltimbocca, or Parmigiana.

Chicken on the bone, either quartered or halved holds up nicely and provides generous portions. Bake the chickens halfway and finish them on the grill for better flavor and appetizing grill marks. Scatter lime wedges over the dish for interest and hands-on dining; guests can squeeze the lime over the grilled chicken themselves. Add a fruit relish, salsa fresca, or other toppings, or shred the chicken for a soft taco.

Heartier meats include lean lamb and pork as well as beef. These respond well to a variety of cooking methods. New economical cuts provide greater versatility and value. The classic loin cut can periodically be substituted with a blade chop or arm chop. It is always important to purchase and receive the best-quality products, recognizing the marks that indicate the different grades and cuts. Well-hung beef is dark red in color and should have a slight marbling of fat throughout for moist, juicy flavor. All of the meat boards and councils are happy to send you information about grading, cuts, recipes, and point-of-sale materials. (See Color Plate 30.)

Refine the presentation of the meat with a few props and garnishes. Again, utilize the meat councils for charts and posters. These materials educate consumers and address controversies.

Try featuring emu, ostrich, buffalo, or game meat as a delicious, interesting, healthy change of pace. The dish can be propped and highlighted with a stuffed small bird on the cough guard shelf. Provide nutritional analyses for health-

Submarines and ships are offering sailors the healthier options of baked or broiled chicken these days. Barbecue night is especially popular. Even if there's no grill on deck, at least the chicken is served with barbecue sauce. Nutritional readouts for the entire menu explain fat grams, calories, carbohydrates, and cholesterol values.

The USS Vicksburg won the 1996 Captain Edward F. Ney Memorial Award for culinary prowess, sanitation, and nutritional offerings. Presentation and arrangements along hot lines are far superior than in days past.

conscious diners and recipes whereby guests can experiment with these foods at home.

Carving stations make a great demonstration area for the cook's slicing expertise. Porterhouse night featuring a ribs option is always popular with the meat-and-potatoes crowd. Cajun rice may be served too, with bits of chicken or beef gravy. Ribs can be layered down the sides of the hotel pan and garnished with a spray of baby corn in the center.

Lamb racks and chine bones are usually garnished with paper crowns. Just for fun, top the bones with glacéed or poached dried apricots. Serve with a Cumberland sauce including dried apricots as part of the recipe for added accord.

✷ TURKEY TENDERLOINS WITH WILD MUSHROOMS MADEIRA

Guests will be impressed with this bit of kitchen or tableside showmanship. Be sure to vary the musky mushroom medley, or add some fresh herbs if you prefer.

YIELD: 16 servings

INGREDIENTS

16 turkey scallops, boned tenderloins, or chicken breasts

2 tablespoons butter (or use spray oil)

2 tablespoons white wine

2 tablespoons oil

6–8 cloves garlic, minced or pressed

6–8 green onions, sliced

3 cups mixed wild mushrooms of choice

1 cup Madeira

Cornstarch to thicken, if desired

INSTRUCTIONS

Pound turkey to a thickness of $1/4$ inch. In a wide frying pan over medium-high heat, melt butter with wine and oil. Pour half the wine mixture into a second sauté pan. Add turkey, skin side down (if retaining), to one pan; add garlic, green onions, and mushrooms to the other. Sauté contents of both pans until turkey is lightly browned, 3–5 minutes per side, and vegetables are tender. Add Madeira to pan with vegetables, shaking pan to distribute. Heat and ignite.

Serve turkey tenderloins with sauce poured over. If necessary, turkey and sauce can be covered and served from hotel pan or chafing dish.

✳ *VARIATION*

If you prefer a coating, dip cutlets in 2 eggs mixed with $1/2$ cup milk, then in flour. Coat just before cooking and shake off excess.

✳ VEAL NORMANDE

Boneless chicken breasts or turkey breast slices pounded to a thickness of $1/4$ inch may be substituted for the more expensive veal. Vegetarians may be served a slab of tofu or tempeh. This is a healthier version of the classic dish from the Normandy region of France, where Calvados—an alcohol distilled from cider—is produced.

YIELD: 16 servings

INGREDIENTS

6 pounds boneless veal in $1/4$-inch-thick slices

2 cups flour

2 tablespoons butter

2 tablespoons oil

1 cup Calvados, apple brandy, or dry white wine

8 tart green apples, cored and thinly sliced

2 cups nonfat sour cream

GARNISH

Minced parsley

(Continued)

INSTRUCTIONS

Place veal between 2 pieces of plastic wrap and pound to a thickness of $^1/_8$ inch. Coat with flour. Shake to remove excess.

Heat chafing dish to keep veal hot. Melt butter with oil in a wide nonstick frying pan over medium heat. Add veal and sauté until lightly browned but still pale pink inside, about 2 minutes per side. Remove to chafing dish.

Add Calvados to frying pan, scraping bottom of pan to free browned bits. Flambé if desired. Add apple slices and sauté 3–5 minutes. Reduce heat, stir in sour cream, and simmer until warm.

Serve veal topped with apple slices and sauce and garnished with parsley.

SELECT SKIRT STEAK OR OSTRICH FAJITAS

YIELD: 24 servings

INGREDIENTS

24 flour or whole-wheat tortillas, 8 inches in diameter

Vegetable cooking spray

6 pounds skirt steak or ostrich fajita strips

$^1/_3$ cup Schrieber's Southwest Seasoning

12 cloves garlic, minced or pressed

1 tablespoon ground cumin

1 tablespoon ground black pepper

$^1/_3$ cup lime juice

1 quart green onions, diagonally sliced

2 cups fresh cilantro, chopped

1 quart plain nonfat yogurt

12 tomatoes

INSTRUCTIONS

Preheat oven to 350°F. Wrap tortillas in damp paper towels and then in aluminum foil. Bake for 7 minutes or until softened; set aside.

Coat a large nonstick skillet with cooking spray; place over medium-high heat until hot. Add meat, Southwest Seasoning, garlic, and cumin; sauté 3–5 minutes or until meat is done. Combine meat, pepper, and lime juice in a bowl and toss well. Add green onions, cilantro, and yogurt and toss well.

Divide meat mixture evenly over tortillas. Cut tomatoes into $\frac{1}{8}$-inch-thick slices (about 4 slices per tomato). Cut each slice in half crosswise. Top each tortilla with 4 tomato pieces; roll up.

✱ SELECT BEEF BURGUNDY STEW

A traditional French dish, burgundy beef stew usually involves simmering the center portion of a chuck roast in a hearty red wine for a rich and tangy taste. For a more exotic version, use ostrich, elk, bear, or venison and serve with small Yukon Gold or red new potatoes. Because this is a make-ahead dish, it can simply be heated and then served from a chafer after the flavors have melded overnight.

YIELD: 16 servings

INGREDIENTS

6 pounds beef tips, ostrich, or venison stewing meat

$\frac{1}{4}$ cup butter or olive oil

2 cups smoked pork shoulder picnic or ham, cut in $\frac{1}{2}$-inch-wide strips

6–8 onions, thinly sliced

6 cloves garlic, minced or pressed

6 medium carrots, cut in $\frac{1}{2}$-inch slices

2 cups parsley, chopped

4 bay leaves

1 tablespoon herbes de Provence (scratch blend or Schrieber's)

1 tablespoon tomato paste

1 quart dry red wine

1 pound mushrooms, sliced

Salt

(Continued)

INSTRUCTIONS

In a large frying pan brown meat well in heated butter. Add ham strips and brown them. Add onions, garlic, carrots, parsley, bay leaves, herbes de Provence, and tomato paste. Stir in wine. Mix in mushrooms and their liquid. Bring just to a boil, reduce heat, cover, and simmer until meat is very tender, about 1 hour. With a slotted spoon, remove meat and vegetables to a serving dish; keep warm.

Bring cooking liquid to a boil and cook, stirring frequently, until reduced and slightly thickened. Salt to taste. Pour over meat and serve.

✴ ANYTIME BARBECUED KEBABS

In years past, marinades were used to tenderize and preserve foods. Today, they are used to add flavor and moisture to foods before cooking. Acidic bases, such as wine, vinegar, citrus, soy sauce, and yogurt, allow marinades to penetrate the food, providing a deep and robust flavor.

The Mediterranean marinade captures the flavors of the Côte d'Azur—fresh basil, lemon, white wine, and lots of garlic. The Indian yogurt marinade is a lowfat blend of aromatic Eastern spices.

Use your imagination to design your own kebabs. Skewer a selection of tender beef tips, emu, or ostrich and vegetables. Marinate, if desired, then grill or broil. Set aside part of the marinade to use as a dipping sauce. Serve with a choice of marinades.

YIELD: 18 servings

INGREDIENTS

VEGETABLES AND FRUITS

1 large onion, cut in chunks

1 large green or red bell pepper, cut in squares

10–12 large mushrooms

8–10 cherry tomatoes

6–8 ears frozen baby corn

8–10 cubes eggplant, zucchini, or crookneck squash

8 small white onions

8 pineapple chunks

MEATS

2 pounds any meat, cut into chunks

MEDITERRANEAN MARINADE

1 cup olive oil	$^{1}/_{4}$ cup fresh basil, chopped
1 cup lemon juice	1 teaspoon salt
1 cup white wine or water	1 teaspoon ground coriander
8 cloves garlic, minced	Freshly ground pepper to taste

INDIAN YOGURT MARINADE

1 cup plain nonfat yogurt	1 teaspoon chili powder
1 small red onion, chopped	$^{1}/_{2}$ teaspoon freshly ground pepper
2 cloves garlic, minced	$^{1}/_{2}$ teaspoon cinnamon
1 tablespoon crystallized ginger, minced	$^{1}/_{4}$ teaspoon ground cloves
$1^{1}/_{2}$ teaspoons cumin	$^{1}/_{4}$ teaspoon ground cardamom
1 teaspoon grated nutmeg	

THREE-CITRUS TERIYAKI SAUCE (see p. 55)

INSTRUCTIONS

Set a heavyweight plastic bag with a resealable zip closure in a bowl and pour marinade into it. Add meat or vegetables and seal. Rock bag gently for even distribution and refrigerate for at least 1 hour; turn bag over halfway through marinating time.

Soak wooden skewers first if grilling. Alternate piercing meats and vegetables for contrast and color.

(Continued)

MEDITERRANEAN MARINADE

Blend all ingredients.

INDIAN YOGURT MARINADE

Blend all ingredients.

PASTA, RICE, AND GRAINS

Pasta is now available in amazing colors and flavors. Ravioli present beautifully at an interactive cold or hot pasta bar. Among the many possibilities are goat cheese triangles in red and white hues, green chili cilantro squares of desert-style painted ravioli, and striped rounds of ravioli filled with lobster and crab (available from Pugliani Pasta). These rainbow pastas add color to any hot or cold line (see Color Plate 31).

Orzo is a popular pasta lately. It almost looks like a long-grain rice and is slightly smaller than a pine nut. Orzo is a wonderful substitute for rice, taking only 5 minutes to cook, and is available in a myriad of colors.

Rices are abundant and always popular. Jasmine rice is a favorite at the Treasure Island Hotel, Las Vegas, yet the chefs prepare many other varieties too. Bulgur or cracked wheat, Kashi, couscous, and quinoa may be served at banquets or on the buffet line. Brown Basmati and California short-grain rice and other nutty whole grains are delicious and make a refreshing change for a good price. Additionally, all of these have good steam table holding capabilities.

Other grains are also worth seeking for a distinctive presentation. Millet, quinoa, triticale, and spelt are all inexpensive and tasty. Some grains cook quickly, such as couscous and quinoa. The latter was a staple of the ancient Incas, who named it "the mother grain." Because it contains all eight essential amino acids, quinoa is considered a complete protein. This supergrain is also higher in unsaturated fats and lower in carbohydrates than most grains and offers a rich source of vital nutrients. For a good food cost, it expands by four times and takes half the cooking time of regular rice. Quinoa is a bit lighter and subtler than rice but can substitute for it or be mixed with millet or other grains. Experiment with these resurgent grains in main and side dishes, soups, and puddings.

Pasta bars, hot and cold, abound in San Antonio. The Hyatt enjoys great success exhibiting Italian cooking during the business person's lunch. Pastas are served in many colors and shapes, and with three sauces that vary weekly. Vegetable, poultry, smoked meat, and seafood medleys all feature tasty local vegetables. Many of the pastas are available hot or cold, depending on the weather.

RAINBOW VEGETABLES

Variety and good nutrition are the important contributions that vegetables make to menus. Variety occurs in flavor, texture, and color for good eating, nutrition in the form of nutrients necessary for good health. Vegetables are a source of vitamins A and C and of important minerals, particularly iron and calcium. Mature dry legumes (peas, beans, and lentils) furnish protein as well as B vitamins and other nutrients. Fortunately, most vegetables are low in calories.

Modern production, transportation, and storage methods make available an abundance of fresh vegetables. Lettuce, tomatoes, cabbage, onions, carrots, and potatoes are among those we can count on buying at any time. Frozen and dried vegetables assure a supply of practically the entire range of varieties.

Fresh vegetables are at their highest quality and lowest price when local and in season. Choose vegetables that look fresh and crisp and have no skin punctures, bruises, or decay. Buy only to the par levels, keep relatively dry, and handle with care. Many fresh vegetables and mixes are washed, trimmed, and packaged, which helps prevent overhandling and preserves freshness. All you need to do is check your labor cost against the price.

★ SAUTÉED VEGETABLE MEDLEY

Vary the baby vegetables and the herbs, and try garnishing them with flowering herbs or edible flowers. Alternatively, marinate them in the Mediterranean marinade (recipe above) and roast in wood-fired oven or on the grill.

YIELD: 16 servings

(Continued)

INGREDIENTS

2 pounds small new Yukon Gold
   potatoes, quartered

48 baby carrots, peeled and topped

16 small white onions, peeled and
   halved

24 baby beets

1 tablespoon butter

$1/4$ cup white wine or broth

24 baby zucchini

24 baby crookneck squash

$1/4$ cup fresh basil, chopped

GARNISH

Grated Parmigana, sapsago, or asiago cheese

INSTRUCTIONS

In a large saucepan of boiling water to cover, cook potatoes for 5 minutes. Add carrots, onions, and beets and cook 5 minutes more. Meanwhile, drop butter and wine or broth into a large heated skillet; add zucchini and crookneck squash and sauté. Drain boiled vegetables, add to skillet, and sauté briefly. Add basil; toss vegetables to mix. Garnish with cheese.

✶ *VARIATION*

Experiment with celery root, parsnips, rutabagas, turnips, leeks, and various fresh herbs.

✶ SWEET POTATO SOUFFLE

This is beautiful served in scalloped or fluted oranges or even grapefruits, for larger portions. The variations listed below add flavor, color, and crunch.

YIELD: 24 servings

INGREDIENTS

24 small sweet potatoes or yams, cooked

3 ounces butter

1 tablespoon salt

Orange juice, to moisten

3 cups canned crushed pineapple, drained

3 cups pecans

$12\frac{1}{2}$ ounces evaporated skim milk, whipped

GARNISH

24 large oranges, scalloped and juiced

INSTRUCTIONS

Whip potatoes until light. Fold in remaining ingredients. Fill fluted orange shells.

✳ *VARIATION*

Add pineapple chunks, diced dates, chopped pecans, or dried cranberries.

✳ EGGPLANT PARMIGIANA

This hearty dish is a vegetarian classic. The sauce goes well with many pasta and egg dishes, so it is sensible to make a double batch. Add a little wheat germ, bran, or even Brewer's Yeast to the crumb mixture for a nutritional boost.

YIELD: 8 servings

(Continued)

INGREDIENTS

2 eggplants, unpeeled

2 eggs

$1/2$ cup skim milk

1 cup flour

1 cup dry bread crumbs or cracker
  meal

$1/4$ cup olive oil

1 pound nonfat mozzarella cheese,
  sliced

Freshly grated Parmesan, Sapsago, or
  shaved Asiago cheese (optional)

PARMIGIANA SAUCE

2 tablespoons olive oil

1 large red onion, chopped

2 garlic cloves, minced

$1/2$ cup yellow bell pepper, diced

$1/2$ cup green bell pepper, diced

2 cans Italian plum tomatoes,
  28 ounces each

$1/4$ cup minced parsley

2 tablespoons mixed fresh basil,
  thyme, and oregano, minced

VERMICELLI

2 quarts water

1 teaspoon salt (optional)

8 ounces vermicelli

INSTRUCTIONS

Wash eggplants and cut into $1/2$-inch-thick slices. Steam over boiling water for 5 minutes. Press each slice firmly between paper towels to remove moisture.

Beat eggs with milk. Coat each slice of eggplant with flour, then with egg-milk mixture, and finally with bread crumbs.

Divide oil between 2 large nonstick frying pans; add eggplant and sauté over medium-high heat until golden brown on both sides. Top each eggplant slice with a cheese slice. Cover pans and cook over low heat until cheese melts, about 5 minutes. Serve on vermicelli, topped with Parmigiana sauce and a sprinkling of Parmesan or other cheese of choice.

PARMIGIANA SAUCE

In a large frying pan, heat oil. Add onion, garlic, and bell peppers and sauté until softened. Add tomatoes and their liquid, breaking up with a fork. Add the parsley and mixed herbs to pan. Simmer, uncovered, until liquid is reduced, 10–15 minutes. Serve sauce over the eggplant.

VERMICELLI

In a large pot, bring the water and optional salt to a boil. Add vermicelli and cook, uncovered, until al dente, 3–5 minutes. Drain.

BAKED MUSHROOMS

This is a great way to experiment with new mushrooms. Try using chanterelles, portobellos, shiitake, porcini, or even wood ear.

YIELD: 16 servings

INGREDIENTS

4 pounds (90 medium) mushrooms

1 cup parsley, minced

$^3/_4$ cup Amontillado dry sherry

Salt and freshly ground pepper

Nonfat sour cream

INSTRUCTIONS

Preheat oven to 450°F. Rinse or lightly brush mushrooms, trim ends, and halve. Place in half or full hotel pan. Top with $^1/_4$ cup of the parsley, sherry, and salt and pepper to taste. Cover with lid and bake until tender, about 20 minutes. Top with dollops of sour cream to coat. Garnish with remaining parsley.

SPINACH MADEIRA MORNAY

Madeira Mornay sauce is delectable on mussels, oysters, pasta, and on its own with spinach and a fluted tomato. Stouffers and Nestle supply high-quality spinach soufflé mixtures and creamed spinach developed for buffets. The spinach that was served in Magic Pan's crepes is easy to make and appealing to the eye in stuffed shells as well.

YIELD: 4 servings

INGREDIENTS

4 ounces frozen chopped spinach,
   thawed

2 ounces Madeira Mornay sauce
   (any classic recipe)

2 tomatoes, cut in half, fluted
   and seeded

GARNISHES

Parmesan or Asiago cheese

Parsley, sprig or minced

Sour cream

INSTRUCTIONS

Mix spinach with Madeira Mornay. Place tomatoes on a sheet pan; bake in convection oven for 10 minutes at 350°F. Heat and hold creamed spinach in steam table. Place $1^1/_2$ ounces creamed spinach on tomato half. Garnish at will.

✳ VARIATION

Serve creamed spinach in an oversized pasta shell.

Root vegetables are excellent choices for all food service segments. Utilize color charts and try new vegetables.

PIZZA

Everyone seems to love pizza, and there is no reason why it cannot go on a hot line right from a wood-burning stove, or convection oven. Pizza can be created to suit just about anyone's taste. Several kid's pizzas were developed for a national chain, including peanut butter and jelly with garnish options of banana chips, raisins, chocolate chips, and marshmallows. The beauty of a pizza is that it is all in the crust and that crust is yet another blank canvas to yield up an art form. The choice of toppings is up to you. The healthful low-fat or decadent dessert pizza is in your hands.

The small conveyor belt ovens are priced reasonably and many things may be cooked within them besides pizza, including plantains, potato chips, marinated vegetables, fish, chicken breasts, cookies, and more. For bread and breakfast operations or home ovens, the key is to use a very hot oven and a pizza stone, preferably dusted with coarse cornmeal or grits (unglazed stones or tiles imitate the lining of a real stone pizza oven; they absorb moisture from the dough, making it crisp, and distribute heat evenly). The next best alternative is to bake pizza on an upside down cookie sheet. Hold pizzas under a hot lamp instead of over steam; they go so fast there won't be time for them to get cold.

Pizza can also be served as an appetizer, entrée, or even a bread side dish or snack. Try cornmeal in the crust for a Southwest pizza; put a scrambled egg on top of spicy crumbled sausage and diced chiles or bell peppers for a breakfast pizza. Making several individual pizzas, rather than one large one, is convenient because they are easier to slide from the pizza peel onto the heated baking stone in the oven.

Main Street Station, Las Vegas, serves a great variety of pizzas for lunch and dinner. They are made fast in a wood-burning oven from mise en place ingredients, stay hot, and sell quickly.

PROVENCE PIZZA ARLESIENNE (BASIC PIZZA)

✱

YIELD: 1 pizza, 9 inches in diameter

INGREDIENTS

1 pizza shell or focaccia

$1/2$ ounce garlic olive oil

2 ounces Pomodora or Parmigiana
sauce

2 ounces mozzarella or Asiago,
shredded

2 ounces roma tomatoes, sliced

1 clove garlic, minced

1 ounce salami, sliced

1 ounce pepperoni, sliced

$1/4$–$1/2$ ounce capers (optional)

Anchovies (optional)

Parsley, minced

INSTRUCTIONS

Place pizza shell on mesh screens or a round pan and brush with garlic olive oil.
Distribute sauce and cheese evenly. Spread tomatoes, garlic, salami, pepperoni, capers, and anchovies evenly across pizza.

Place pizza on conveyor belt in 450°F oven, wood burning oven, or convection
oven and cook 6–8 minutes. For a home oven, cook for 12–15 minutes at 450°F,
depending upon your calibration (until golden brown and bubbly). Sprinkle pizza
with minced parsley before serving.

✱ MEDITERRANEAN PIZZA

Prepare the basic pizza clear to the sauce, cheese, tomatoes, and garlic stage,
but with no "option" on the capers and anchovies; it is a must-have for
Mediterranean cuisine. Spread 2 ounces of quartered marinated artichokes,
$1^1/2$ ounces julienned colored bell peppers evenly across pizza. Sprinkle with
1 tablespoon freshly chopped basil and 1 tablespoon rosemary just before
serving.

✳ *TRENDY CHIC CALIFORNIA PIZZA*

I developed this concept for Cal-a-Vie Spa in California. I shared it and other culinary concepts with pizza operators and aficionados at the First Annual Italian-American Foodservice Show in October, 1994 in Las Vegas, where I was a judge and demonstrator. The key to the pizza is that it is delicious and low in fat, calories, and cholesterol. Prepare the basic pizza but substitute 2 ounces of sparkling roasted red pepper puree (see recipe in Chapter 3) instead of pizza sauce. Then spread 2 ounces of Mozzarella and Asiago or Parmesan mix, 1 ounce of caramelized red onions, and 2 ounces sliced portabello mushrooms into elongated strips evenly across pizza. Sprinkle 1 ounce crumbled goat cheese, $1^1/_2$ ounces julienned colored bell peppers, and $1^1/_2$ ounce pinenuts evenly over pizza. Scatter 1 tablespoon cut chiffonade of basil and 1 tablespoon minced parsley just before serving.

✳ *ITALIAN CAPRICCIOSA PIZZA*

Prepare the basic pizza but substitute 2 ounces of pesto sauce instead of pizza sauce. Then top 2 ounces of Mozzarella & Romano mix, 1 ounce thinly sliced Serrano, Parma, or a dry cured quality ham, 1 ounce sliced salami, 2 ounces quartered, marinated artichoke hearts, and $^1/_2$ ounce sliced kalamata olives evenly across pizza. Scatter minced Italian parsley as needed to garnish, just before serving.

✳ *ROASTED LEMON CHICKEN PIZZA*

Prepare basic pizza but substitute 3 ounces of Marinara sauce for the pizza sauce and $^1/_2$ ounce roasted garlic puree and 3 ounces of Mozzarella and Asiago cheese mix evenly. Spread 3 ounces roasted lemon chicken slices, $^1/_8$ ounce of capers, $1^1/_2$ ounces julienned green pepper, and $1^1/_2$ ounces julienned yellow squash evenly across pizza. Garnish with a chiffonade of basil and minced parsley as needed and serve on pizza platter.

✳ *PIZZA AU FUNGHI*

Prepare as above but brush with $^1/_2$ ounce of garlic olive oil and 1 ounce of Marinara sauce and 1 ounce of sparkling roasted red pepper puree. Spread 1 ounce sliced portabellos, 1 ounce sliced crimini, and 1 ounce sliced button mushrooms. Scatter $^1/_4$ ounce thinly sliced green onion and $^1/_2$ ounce diced proscuitto on top. Garnish with minced parsley as needed just before serving.

✳ *SOUTHWESTERN BARBECUE CHICKEN PIZZA*

Prepare basic pizza but with 1 ounce Southwest Barbecue sauce (see recipe in Chapter 3) mixed with $^1/_2$ ounce pizza sauce and spread evenly over pizza shell or focaccia. Top evenly with 2 ounces grilled chicken fingers, $^1/_4$ ounce caramelized onions, $^1/_2$ ounce sliced mushrooms (of choice), 2 ounces (4 slices) sliced Roma tomatoes and $1^1/_2$ ounces shredded Mozzarella and Asiago mix.

✳ *TERIYAKI CHICKEN PIZZA*

Prepare basic pizza but use $1^1/_2$ ounces 3-Citrus Teriyaki sauce (see recipe in Chapter 3) for pizza sauce spread evenly over pizza shell or focaccia. Top evenly with 2 ounces grilled chicken fingers (or pre-cooked lemon chicken), $^1/_4$ ounce caramelized onions, $^1/_2$ ounce sliced mushrooms, and $1^1/_2$ ounces Mozzarella and Parmesan, Romano, or Asiago mixed.

✳ BRUSCHETTA SALAD WITH GRILLED VEGETABLES

YIELD: 1 serving

INGREDIENTS

1 focaccia, $5^1/_2$ inches square, split

1 ounce red pepper purée

1 ounce portobello mushrooms, sliced lengthwise

1 ounce crookneck squash, sliced lengthwise

1 ounce zucchini, sliced lengthwise

$^1/_2$ ounce mixed bell peppers, cut julienne

$^1/_2$ clove garlic, minced

1 tablespoon oregano

1 tablespoon olive oil

1 tablespoon balsamic vinegar

2 ounces mista mix of organic baby lettuces

1 ounce mild goat cheese, crumbled

1 ounce feta cheese, crumbled

1 ounce lemon vinaigrette

Pine nuts (optional)

INSTRUCTIONS

Toast focaccia in a 450° oven, wood burning oven, or convection oven for 3 minutes. Grill all vegetables, except for mista mix, in a wood burning oven or pizza oven for 3–5 minutes, or grill over an open flame. Spread focaccia with pepper puree, grilled vegetables, garlic, oregano, olive oil, balsamic vinegar, mista mix, and crumbled cheeses. Serve focaccia in a sandwich basket with lemon vinaigrette on the side in a ramekin.

NORTHWEST BERRY DESSERT PIZZA

This dessert pizza which I demonstrated in Las Vegas at a national competition, was intriguing to many pizza owners despite the volume and variety of entries.

Below the colorful medley of fruits are a creamy sweet surprise and the crunch of nuts in the crust. The citrus cream filling is made of cream cheese, sour cream, and ricotta, all nonfat.

YIELD: 4 tarts, 10–12 inches in diameter

INGREDIENTS

LINZERTORTE PIZZA CRUST

4 sticks butter, softened

$\frac{1}{2}$ cup honey or sugar

4 egg yolks

4 cups all-purpose flour

2 cups walnuts, chopped

2 cups almonds or hazelnuts, chopped

2 teaspoons ground ginger

2 teaspoons cinnamon

2 teaspoons nutmeg, grated

(Continued)

NONFAT THREE-CITRUS CREAM FILLING

2 pounds nonfat cream cheese

1 cup nonfat ricotta

1 cup nonfat sour cream

Rind of 2 oranges, grated

Rind of 2 limes, grated

Rind of 2 lemons, grated

$1/2$–$2/3$ cup honey

$1/2$ cup orange juice

FRUIT LAYER

3 quarts mixed berries, such as yellow raspberries, huckleberries, blackberries, and blueberries, optional sliced kiwi and starfruit

$2/3$ cup orange marmalade or apricot preserves

$2/3$ cup red currant jelly or raspberry jelly

$1/3$–$1/2$ cup lemon juice

$1/4$ cup orange liqueur (optional)

GARNISHES

Mint sprigs

Candied violets

Crystallized grapes

Spun sugar

INSTRUCTIONS

LINZERTORTE PIZZA CRUST

Cream butter and honey. Beat in egg yolks. Mix in flour, walnuts, almonds, ginger, cinnamon, and nutmeg. Roll out dough and line four 10- to 12-inch tart or quiche pans. Place crusts in refrigerator or freezer until thoroughly chilled.

Preheat oven to 375°F. Bake crusts for 15–20 minutes; cool.

NONFAT THREE-CITRUS CREAM FILLING

Combine all ingredients and whip in a processor fitted with a plastic blade or in an electric mixer until light and creamy. Fill baked and cooled crusts with filling.

FRUIT LAYER

Top filled crust with berries in any pattern. Select preserves based on predominant berry colors; choose orange for golden berries, red for darker berries. In saucepan, heat selected marmalade and jelly; stir in lemon juice and liqueur. Brush this glaze over berries.

GARNISHES

Garnish at will. Serve at room temperature.

CREDITS

Bally's Las Vegas
Color Plate 17

David Burch
Color Plates 2, 9, 10, 18, 22, 23, 27, 28, 29, 30, and 31

Cole Publishing Group, Inc.
Color Plates 3, 8, and 24. Copyright Cole Publishing Group, Inc. All rights reserved. Used by permission.

Linda Fabrizius
Line drawings

Fresh Choice/Zoopa Restaurants
Color Plate 13

Paula Johnson
Model for Color Plate 12

Robert Johnson
Cover photo and Color Plates 1, 5, 6, 7, 12, 14, 15, 16, 21, and 25

Daniel L. Jones
Model for Color Plate 16

Deni Linhart
Color Plates 4, 11, 19, 20, and 26

Morris Wolf
Color Plate 32. © Morris Wolf Photography.

Jesse Yoshida
Model for Color Plate 25

INDEX